TIPPERARY &
WATERFORD

A Walking Guide

JOHN G. O'DWYER works as a travel consultant and also teaches tourism and business to further education students. A keen hillwalker and rock climber, he is a founder member of Mid-Tipp Hillwalkers and has almost twenty-five years' experience of leading hillwalking and mountain-climbing groups in Ireland, the UK, Europe and Africa.

Devil's Bit

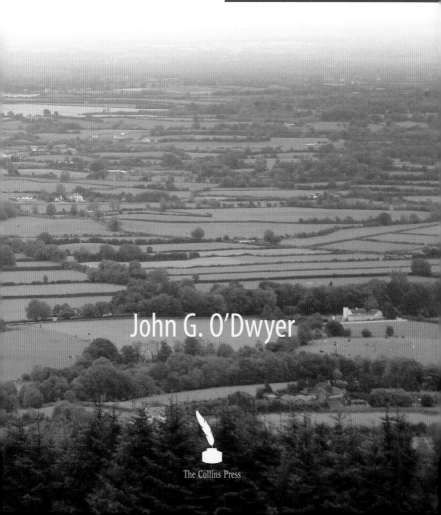

TIPPERARY &
WATERFORD

A Walking Guide

John G. O'Dwyer

The Collins Press

FIRST PUBLISHED IN 2012 BY
The Collins Press
West Link Park
Doughcloyne
Wilton
Cork

British Library Cataloguing in Publication Data

O'Dwyer, John G.

Tipperary & Waterford : a walking guide.
1. Walking¬—Ireland—Tipperary (County)—Guidebooks.
2. Walking—Ireland—Waterford (County)—Guidebooks.
3. Tipperary (Ireland : County)—Guidebooks. 4. Waterford
(Ireland : County)—Guidebooks.
I. Title
796.5'1'094191-dc23

ISBN: 9781848891449

Design and typesetting by Fairways Design

Typeset in Avenir

Printed in Poland by Białostockie Zakłady Graficzne SA

Contents

THE ARRA MOUNTAINS

OTHER WALKS

View from Knocknafallia summit cairn to Knockmealdown Mountain

Introduction

They just can't just help it: mountains are natural attention-grabbers. Great peaks exert a magnetic pull, drawing the eye to the highest place where legend traditionally sites the abode of demons and deities. The forbidding summits of the world's great mountains, such as Kilimanjaro, Olympus and Everest, have evoked equal measures of fear and reverence among upward-gazing people. Most often they were seen as malevolent places, with early climbers commonly regarded as reckless tempters of fate.

But size is not everything when it comes to mountains and this is particularly the case with the east Munster uplands. There is no mountain in the area that cannot be reached on a good day by a reasonably fit walker, using nothing more technical than sustained legwork. It is no wonder that the summits of Tipperary and Waterford have not become distant objects of reverence and fear but rather comforting parts of the landscape that have often been purposefully woven into the myths and legends used to bind communities since pre-Christian times.

Like ageing divas, however, mountains may appear to show their best side to the uninitiated when appreciated from afar. Romantic tales are most alluring when the diva or the hill is far away – on stage or horizon. Get closer and the magic may at first be lessened.

Most of the east Munster mountain ranges consist of rounded peaks or undulating plateaus that can be cold, windy and eroded, while very often mist obscures the wished-for view. So those who come to these highlands with a vision informed by the idealised paintings of the Romantic period are almost certainly bound for disappointment. And it is not just the weather or the terrain that may spoil the romance, but also the work of man.

Human influence is everywhere. There are trig points, sculptures, deflector masts, tombs, crosses, altars, towers, huts, shelters and, of course, the ubiquitous cairns. The historic, the aesthetic, the commercial and the spiritual all jostle for the psychological dominance offered by the highest summits.

But this should not be off-putting, for wilderness – when defined as landscape unaltered by human intervention – exists nowhere on this island and those who seek it are likely to remain unfulfilled. Every Irish landscape – from brook to beach, mountain to marsh, hedge to heath – is shaped by human intervention.

Just as a seascape is enhanced by a scrap of sail and a lowland meadow by gambolling horseflesh, the upland experience is at its most rewarding when we come to understand how high places have contributed to human endeavour by seeking out and understanding the clues in the landscape. A booley in a high place tells a tale of contribution to human survival; a working farmstead on a mountainside demonstrates the success of this contribution; a ruined cottage confirms a battle lost. Politically, economically or spiritually – depending on perceived need – the powerful symbolism and economic value of our mountains have been exploited historically to sustain and bind communities.

It is inescapable: no matter where you wander, the highlands of Waterford and Tipperary are loaded with history and legend. The secret is to do a little research before you ascend. Then press the pause button on your frenetic 21st-century life while you head out among the ancient, much weathered hills of East Munster and see the landscape spring to life as an ornately illustrated storybook. You will most likely return enriched and invigorated by your upland experience and already looking forward to your next hill-country outing – for once established, a walking habit is a gift that keeps on giving.

Safety on the hills

This spirit of adventure lurks somewhere within us all. It is this pursuit of challenge and uncertainty that drives us forward to seek higher planes of endeavour and to push back the frontiers of the possible. It finds expression in the successes of Amundsen and Hillary, in the failures of Mallory and Scott – and within every hillwalker who struggles bravely to reach a modest Irish hilltop.

All very worthwhile and challenging, of course, assuming that, unlike Mallory and Scott, everyone comes back in one piece. While it is statistically true that the most dangerous part of any climb is the road journey to the trailhead, it should, nevertheless, be kept in mind that accidents do happen in the hill country, and they mostly occur when and where we least expect them.

Hillwalkers come to grief more often on easy slopes or very commonly in that moment of relaxation at the end of a hard climb. The descent is also a prime time when climbers snatch defeat from the jaws of victory, since this is when we are generally more tired, less watchful and subconsciously feel the day's work is done. Nonetheless, those whose first experience of our high country comes on a cloudless, benign day will wonder – despite much evidence to the contrary – how we can possibly have so many mountain accidents, and even fatalities.

The answer is, of course, that while in Spain the rain may indeed fall mainly on the plain, in Ireland it falls predominantly on the uplands with the result that there are many days of low cloud, breath-robbing gales and louring drizzle. Without direct experience, its hard to imagine how – since Irish mountains aren't very high – the weather on the peaks can be so different from that at sea level. It is all too easy to get caught out, unprepared for the conditions, and the consequences can range from uncomfortable to desperately serious. The forecast for Cahir may be for a 20km/h breeze and temperature of 10 °C: on Galtymore summit this could mean -5 °C and gusts of 70km/h.

Distant views of mountains speak tantalisingly of freedom and adventure, but seldom hint towards the hardships and dangers that can lie in wait. This has been the downfall of many. So if we want to climb among even the modest Irish mountains we must expect rain as often as sunshine, storms as well as gentle breezes, and all-obscuring drizzle as frequently as magical moments.

The first rule of mountain safety is to be adequately clothed. Not only is it pleasanter to be warm and dry, it is a lot safer since we function much better when we are comfortable. The adage, 'if your feet are cold put on a hat', has much to commend it. For many hillwalkers, a hat is the item of clothing not to be without, since it is so light to carry and the uncovered head accounts for half the body's heat loss. Of course, there is also a need for full body cover and when heading up onto the higher summits we should also have a waterproof jacket, a fleece, overtrousers, and two pairs of gloves.

The second rule is to carry sufficient food and a warm drink since hillwalking is in an extremely strenuous activity. It is also prudent to bring along some emergency rations in case you get delayed or benighted. For this purpose carbohydrates are best as they are easiest for your body to convert quickly into energy. Finally, carry a mobile phone as a backup but do not rely on it totally – Murphy's Law suggests it won't work at the time you most need it.

The final rule is to remember that having a map and compass in your rucksack is about as useful for route finding as a desert lighthouse unless you know how to navigate. So learn to route find competently in mist if you intend having recourse to the high summits. Otherwise, stick with walks that offer a navigational handrail. These can be the cliff tops above a coum as at Coumshingaun, a continuous fence similar to the many that exist in the west Knockmealdowns or a well-defined mountain track such as that leading to Lough Muskry in the Galtee Mountains.

So, if the hillwalking bug has recently bitten you, give the hard-working volunteers from the South East Mountain Rescue Team a break by taking some of the basic safety precautions listed above. Remember, the hills should foster our spirit of self-reliance. When planning a mountain walk there are some basic questions to be answered.

- Do you know where you are going and have you the navigational skills to get there and back in poor visibility?
- Have you estimated how long the walk will take?
- Are you sure it is within your ability and that of your companions to complete it safely with time to spare before nightfall?
- Finally, does someone know your intended route and estimated time of return?

If the answer is 'yes' to these questions, you are now set for memorable and rewarding days in the mountains of Tipperary and Waterford.

Panoramic view of Mauherslieve

SLIEVEFELIM WALKS

You have been a low-level walker for some time and your fitness has improved. Now you're ready to move on and a little voice is whispering, 'what next?' You know these voices can only be silenced by more of a challenge – capturing your very own mountaintop, perhaps – but you are not ready yet for navigating the often trackless moorland of the high Galtees and Comeraghs.

Don't let this be a worry, for in these circumstances you can find just the challenge you want amid the captivating charm of the – until recently – little-known Slievefelim Hills. The attraction of these gentle North Tipperary uplands is that, compared with their south-county counterparts, they are on a different, more intimate scale and do not make the less-experienced walker feel insignificant or out of place. The Slievefelim are a patchwork of small fields, woodlands, serene villages and moorland tops and an area where a strong sense of localism still flourishes among the inhabitants. Humans fit in naturally even on the highest summits, which are reached by well-marked trails through a landscape littered with abundant historic artefacts to capture your curiosity and stretch your imagination.

WALK 1
KILCOMMON PILGRIM LOOP AND MAUHERSLIEVE

START:

From Limerick take the N7 for Dublin and then the R503, signposted Newport. Continue through the villages of Newport and Rear Cross until the Cross Bar appears on the left. Go left immediately onto a minor road that leads directly to Kilcommon village. The trailhead is outside the community centre where there is ample parking.

Time:

Allow 2 hours to complete the loop and another 1½ hours to ascend Mauherslieve.

Map:

OSi Sheet 59.

Suitability:

This is an easy route following well-maintained tracks with a total ascent of just 170m. It is, however, wet in places around the Bilboa River so good boots are a definite requirement.

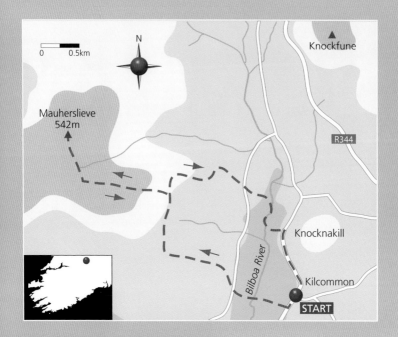

Kilcommon Pilgrim Loop

A feature of the modern life is a phenomenon known as 'the death of distance'. Railways, cars and latterly airplanes have now shrunk our planet to a size where we can travel almost anywhere worldwide within about forty-eight hours. As denizens of this global village we are apt to forget that, not so long ago, a night spent away from home was rare indeed and the limit of most journeys was a half day's walk from one's fireside. But for those who did travel, the slow pace carried its own reward – a deep interaction with the landscape that is impossible nowadays as we hurtle past at 100km/h.

The Pilgrim Trail, developed under the admirable 'Walks Scheme', resurrects ancient paths above the deeply rural village of Kilcommon, which were stoically footed by generations of upland dwellers unencumbered by the demands of wealth and materialism. In those harsher times distances were very real indeed and the next valley often seemed like another country. In fact, the first paved road was completed to the area only in 1831. According to local priest Fr Dan Woods, who has an abiding passion for the history and folklore of Slievefelim, these Mass paths 'not only helped maintain an unbroken chain of faith in the area before the arrival of roads', they also provided a lifeline for all other commercial interactions.

On arrival at the trailhead at **R901 600** it will immediately be clear that this is a captivating trail with abundant aces up its bucolic sleeve. Set in the valley of the Bilboa River and surrounded on all sides by uplands, Kilcommon is a neatly maintained village that valiantly retains its 'olde worlde' charm. First to capture

Led by Con Ryan of Upperchurch and Fr Dan Woods of Kilcommon,
walkers stride out on the Pilgrim Loop

your curiosity will most likely be Kilcommon's pleasingly laid-out prayer garden where a long-standing tradition of pilgrimage continues unabated, with thousands of the faithful still gathering here on summer Sundays.

Initially the route goes left from outside Kilcommon Community Centre to follow a minor road for a short distance before it breaks right to traverse low-lying lands adjacent to the Bilboa River. In summer the fields and lanes here are replete with the rich aromas of the land and walking is pleasant, for every effort has been made to ease your passage. Just follow the purple arrows over locally constructed bridges, which fit snugly into the landscape, and on paths where modern eco-grid has also been laid to consolidate the earth beneath your boots. This is all in the interests of conservation because much of the route passes through an SAC (Special Area of Conservation), which is a local initiative to protect this fragile ecosystem.

When a tarmac roadway is reached go right and soon after make a left to join a woodland track that swings right before continuing to reach a forestry roadway. A right turn here and you are soon traversing the lower skirts of deeply mythological Mauherslieve ('mother mountain') – a shy mountain that for the most part blushes unsung and unvisited. This decidedly feminine mountain is referred to by local people as Moher Clea and was reputedly in pre-Christian times an abode of the pagan goddess Eibhleen. After about a kilometre you are given a choice to foot it upwards on a more demanding track to Mauherslieve's lonesome crest.

To do this, follow an arrow that points left into a dense forest. Continue following the waymarkers through the forest to reach open mountain and then upwards again to reach the shoulder of Mauherslieve. Here the trail swings right and ascends without further incident to the summit (543m) – after about one hour's walk from the Pilgrim Trail. The top is crowned by a large ancient burial cairn, surmounted incongruously by the almost inevitable trig point.

Clearly the builder of this cairn wanted to emphasise its importance by using the powerful imagery of the most elevated place to evoke the reverence and respect of those residing in the valleys below. Mauherslieve was well chosen, as it is a centrally situated summit offering a great vista over the surrounding ring of hills and was until relatively recently the scene of a devotional pattern-day pilgrimage on 29 June each year. For me the view is redolent of (but in many ways more impressive than) that offered by Armagh's famous ring dyke around Slieve Gullion.

Return by your route of ascent to rejoin the Pilgrim Trail and resume following the purple arrows. Leaving the forest you descend through a field to reach a roadway. The arrows point left here, but a 200m detour (right) through a gateway takes you to an ancient Mass rock. This is the perfect place to ignite your

An ancient Mass rock lying just off the Pilgrim Loop

imagination and picture simple but devout people, whose lives were regulated not by clocks but by the rhythms of the countryside, coming from the surrounding hills to kneel and pray on the rough, wet grass while lookouts watched for hostile forces.

The remainder of the route follows the quiet lanes and small fields once so typical of pre-EU, rural Ireland. Along the way you will pass modest but neat farmhouses that have been maintained in a pleasingly vernacular style. Initially it is downhill along a by-road before crossing a field and another road to traverse wettish lands and pass over the Bilboa River once again. Your walk concludes with a 700m ramble along a quiet road past a small riverside park to the trailhead in Kilcommon village.

WALK 2
EAMONN A CHNOIC LOOP

START:
From Thurles follow the R498 (Nenagh road) for about 2km. At a junction for Limerick take the R503 for 13km to a crossroads with a fingerpost (right) for Upperchurch. The village is 500m from here.

Time:
The loop is about 8km in length and should be comfortably completed in about 2½ hours.

Map:
OSi Sheet 59.

Suitability:
The Eamonn a Chnoic Loop is generally unstrenuous, traversing minor roads, laneways and fields, with just 150m of ascent. The route can be muddy in places so walking boots are essential. The walk crosses worked agricultural land, so leave the dog at home, do not disturb farm animals and generally try to minimise your environmental footprint.

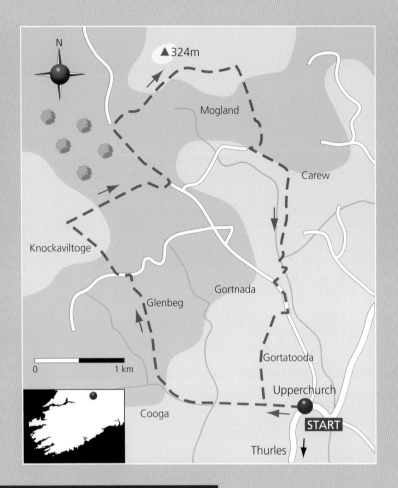

Our most compelling landscapes are not necessarily the most pristine and unaltered. Indeed, the Irish countryside can be at its most captivating where it works hardest for a living. Nowhere is this more apparent than in the landscape north of Upperchurch village in County Tipperary where an innovative approach to recreational walking in Ireland was originally piloted. With freedom of access granted by twenty-three local farmers, this easy but captivating loop meanders through wildflower-rich meadows of working farms and rustic bridleways filled with birdsong and the evocative aromas of the countryside.

This is a corner of Ireland where the environmental mischief-making of the EU Common Agricultural Policy never really built a head of steam. The timeless

Walkers rambling the Upperchurch countryside on the Eamonn a Chnoic Loop

landscape of small fields, luxuriant hedgerows and diverse habitats has somehow survived the onslaught of globalised food production. And if you wish to make it so, this area can be a true wellspring for the imagination, for with just a small step of imagining, mountainy men are once again working the fields with horse-drawn ploughs while cows stand placid and content to be hand-milked on summer evenings. Certainly it is a peaceful environment where a chance encounter with a local is a welcome event. Treat it as an opportunity to discover something about the rich folklore of the area and the renowned Upperchurch welcome will be yours for the taking.

To follow the loop that honours Eamonn a Chnoic – a local rapparee in the Robin Hood tradition – take the road from the trailhead in Upperchurch village **R987 612** that passes the community centre and a childcare facility. After about 10 minutes you reach a bridge. Just beyond, use the stile on your right to enter a field and climb through a series of meadows with linking stiles. At the crest of the ascent you emerge on a roadway and go left.

After 100m, divert right onto a track and then cross a stile to join a green road that leads into a field. Then go right and left to exit the field over a stile and join a bucolic laneway.

This lane takes you downhill by the right-hand side of a house to a public road. Go left here, following the tarmac for 300m before swinging right at a small hay barn. Now enjoy the splendid quietude of the upland countryside as you tag a green road until the route crosses a stile and hugs the edge of a plantation. When you reach the end of the trees turn right and descend by following the walking arrows through a series of fields to reach yet another laneway.

Go left here and then right over a stile and cross fields and a couple of tiny steams before exiting onto a public road where the route is left. After 100m the walking signs point to a laneway on the right. Now it is plain trailing all the way as you cross a stile and continue through a field to reach Church Bog, which is being developed by the local community as a wildlife habitat.

Leave the bog via the wooden gate to the public road, turn left and enjoy a pleasant 300m stroll back to the warm hospitality of three-pub Upperchurch village.

Upperchurch village

WALK 3
KEEPER HILL
(SLIEVEKIMALTA)

START:
From the Tipperary village of Newport take the road
signposted Nenagh. After a short distance swing right at a
graveyard and continue to a crossroads where a fingerpost
for Keeper Trailhead points left. Follow a series of these signs
on small roads to Doonane car park.

Time:
Allow about 3½ hours to complete Keeper Hill and the
Ballyhourigan Loop.

Map:
OSi Sheet 59.

Suitability:
Route follows well-maintained tracks. Venture off track,
however, and the terrain often becomes challenging.

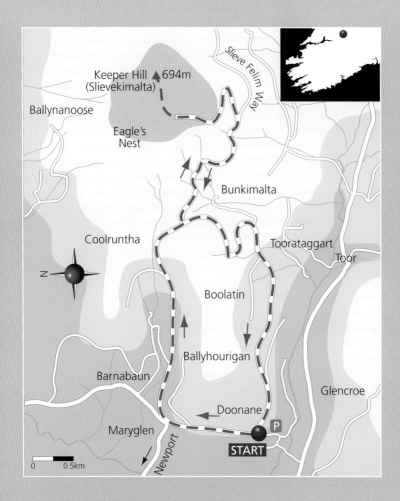

Keeper Hill

The highest mountain in the Shannon Region presides over an area where communities have, for centuries, displayed a doughty independence, spawning rebels and writers in equal measure. Keeper Hill looked down impassively as the seventeenth-century rapparee Galloping Hogan passed beneath at the head of Patrick Sarsfield's men, on an audacious mission to destroy a Limerick-bound siege train.

It watched Eamonn a Chnoic – a local-born outlaw – sally forth on a one-man mission to improve social cohesion by forcefully transferring income from

Keeper Hill

haves to have-nots. He also reputedly found time to pen the epic poem *Seán Ó Duibhir an Ghleanna* and remains the only Irish outlaw to be commemorated with a memorial, which now stands at Curraheen near Hollyford village.

And it was in the last century that writer and uncompromising revolutionary Ernie O'Malley chanced into Keeper's shadow at the head of Munster's 2nd Southern Division, IRA. Here he led attacks by local activists on the nearby

Hollyford and Rearcross RIC Barracks and at one time commanded 7,000 volunteers in the area.

These days Slievefelim is more famous for the enduring strength and vibrancy of its community initiatives with people also coming year round to avail of an excellent network of trails developed by admirable local enterprise.

Sooner or later, however, most visitors will be drawn to the great whaleback mountain that towers imperiously above the surrounding hills. Despite this impressive outline and 694m altitude, Keeper is actually a rather benign beast.

The ascent can prove physically demanding, but otherwise it represents 'hillwalking-lite' as the summit is accessed by a reassuringly well-marked track.

Your walk to the summit of Keeper Hill starts from the well-appointed Doonane car park **R781 652** (see panel above) where you follow the red arrows uphill for about 1.5km to Ballyhourigan Wood. Here, you follow the forest track east for about 3km until it swings south beneath a prominent outcrop known as the Eagle's Nest to reach a three-way junction.

Join the Slievefelim Way by taking the left option and continue beneath an eye-catching gully and then a serene waterfall before the trail begins contouring the south face of the mountain.

When the forest clears on the right, immense vistas will open over the tiny village of Toor, with a line of low hills farther south and, beyond these, the great sweep of the Galtee Mountains.

Soon afterwards you will part company with the Slievefelim Way by following the red walking arrows upwards to the left. This much-improved path now leads to the summit by a circuitous, but not overly steep, route. Along the way there are glimpses of Slievenamon, the Blackstairs Range and the distant Wicklow Mountains.

The summit contains the almost obligatory cairn and trig point along with a huge and decidedly non-obligatory communication mast. The intoxicating vista over the north Tipperary hills to the distant Slieve Bloom Mountains provides adequate compensation, however, for such intrusion.

Descend initially by the same route and then, on a clear day with the vegetation thickening once again you will notice to the west an arc of distant hills. You may initially wonder as to the location of these ranges and then be surprised to figure out that these mountains can only be located in far away west Cork and Kerry.

First to enter your line of vision will most likely be the somewhat suggestive shape of the Paps Mountains. Then further west you will spy Mangerton, and next the unmistakably angular peaks of the MacGillycuddy's Reeks. The Slievemish lie further north and beyond, and seemingly isolated in the silvery western ocean is the sharp outline of the Brandon Ridge.

Eventually you must drag yourself away from the view and descend to the three-way junction encountered earlier. Now follow the blue arrows of the Ballyhourigan Loop instead of retracing your steps to Ballyhourigan Wood, for easy going on a well-signed trail with the fertile patchwork of the renowned Golden Vale laid out below.

When you reach a three-way junction swing left for the short stroll downhill to Doonane while perhaps reflecting on the relative insignificance of our island where even innocuous Keeper Hill offers vistas that encompass virtually the entire south of Ireland.

Overleaf: *Wildflowers adorning the flanks of Keeper Hill*

WALK 4
THE KNOCKALOUGH LOOP

START:
From Thurles take the R498 Nenagh road for 2km. At the junction, signposted Limerick, take the R503 and continue for about 13km to a crossroads with a fingerpost (right) for Upperchurch. Go left instead and you will come to the Knockalough Trailhead after about 500m.

Time:
The distance is about 10km and should be completed comfortably in 3 hours.

Map:
OSi Sheet 66*.

Suitability:
While completing the Knockalough Loop does not exactly involve 'touching the void', it can still be a strenuous ascent and is exposed to the elements in places. So bring warm clothing and raingear, follow the purple arrows and do not stray from the marked route.

* The OSi map is not very clear on detail, however, so if you would like to carry a map, it is better to use the one available from the Upperchurch Community Centre, tel. 0504 54443.

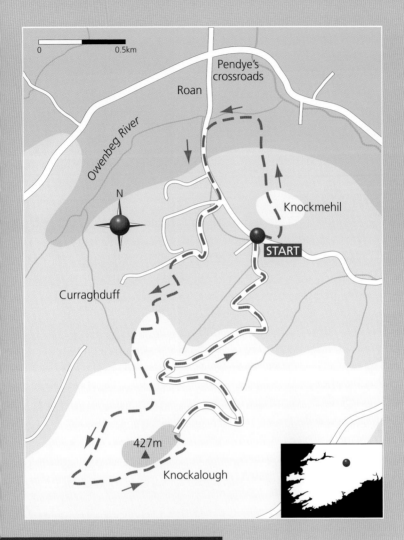

0 0.5km

Pendye's crossroads

Roan

Owenbeg River

N

Knockmehil

START

Curraghduff

427m

Knockalough

The Knockalough Loop

Communities, it is often said, are dense networks of human interactions accompanied by a strong sense of place and certainly there seems to be something in the air around the tiny parish of Upperchurch that breeds altruistic endeavour. For decades now, a group of individuals has worked tirelessly and unremunerated to make the area a byword for proactive rural development. Latterly they have been justly rewarded, with 'Brand Upperchurch' acquiring a muscular appeal that

The view from Knockalough over Upperchurch village to the Slievefelim Hills

Walkers enjoying the Knockalough Loop

Panoramic view of Knockalough

attracts improbably large numbers of visitors for even innocuous local events. One result of this unstinting local endeavour is that this tiny upland community now boasts four excellent walking trails with each telling a different story.

Of these, the Knockalough Loop reaches the highest elevation and offers an opportunity to walk arm-in-arm with the ghosts of history for this is an area associated with the tragic southward journey of Red Hugh O'Donnell – the last of the great Ulster chieftains. He chanced this way on his heroic but ultimately catastrophic march to defeat at the Battle of Kinsale that forever ended Ireland's Gaelic way of life.

Starting the Knockalough Loop from the forestry entrance (see panel above) at **R988 596** cross the road and climb the stile, following the purple arrows. The first section of the loop takes you through pleasant pastures to exit at a surfaced road where you turn left. Follow the surfaced road to reach the entrance to a farmyard on your right.

From here keep right of a farm building and continue for about 600m on a farm roadway to reach a stile on your left where you enter a field and ascend. At the corner of the field go right and follow the hedge to the next corner where you turn left and climb again. After 100m you turn right at two gates – crossing a stile and joining a rustic trail alongside a forestry plantation. Follow this to reach a stile at the entrance to a wood. Now ascend steeply by the edge of woodland to exit onto a forestry service road where you turn right.

Follow this roadway around the edge of forestry as it runs close by but does not actually bring you to the summit proper (427m), which is secreted in woodland. Nevertheless, marvellous views open here to the west across the bewitching bleakness of the Slievefelim highlands to the crowning glories of Mauherslieve and Keeper Hill adorning the western horizon.

When you reach a T-junction with another forestry road turn left. After another 100m go right to begin the descent to the trailhead. Now it is just a matter of continuing to follow the forestry road and directional arrows downhill to reach the trailhead.

Mahon Falls

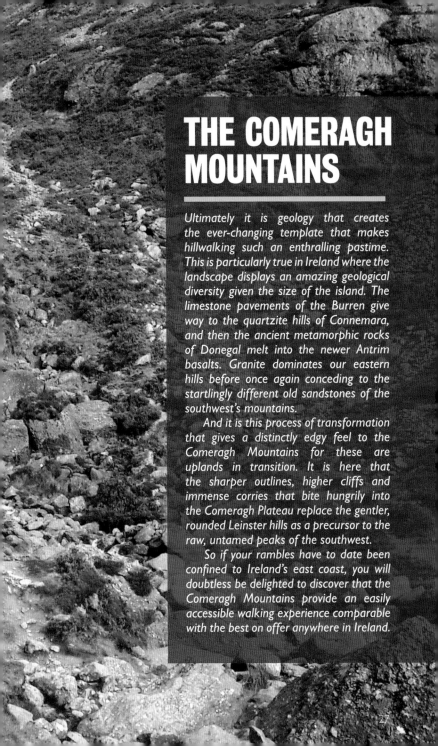

THE COMERAGH MOUNTAINS

Ultimately it is geology that creates the ever-changing template that makes hillwalking such an enthralling pastime. This is particularly true in Ireland where the landscape displays an amazing geological diversity given the size of the island. The limestone pavements of the Burren give way to the quartzite hills of Connemara, and then the ancient metamorphic rocks of Donegal melt into the newer Antrim basalts. Granite dominates our eastern hills before once again conceding to the startlingly different old sandstones of the southwest's mountains.

And it is this process of transformation that gives a distinctly edgy feel to the Comeragh Mountains for these are uplands in transition. It is here that the sharper outlines, higher cliffs and immense corries that bite hungrily into the Comeragh Plateau replace the gentler, rounded Leinster hills as a precursor to the raw, untamed peaks of the southwest.

So if your rambles have to date been confined to Ireland's east coast, you will doubtless be delighted to discover that the Comeragh Mountains provide an easily accessible walking experience comparable with the best on offer anywhere in Ireland.

WALK 5
THE NIRE VALLEY COUMS

START:
From Clonmel, take the R671 Dungarvan road to the County
Waterford village of Ballymacarberry. Turn left at Melody's pub
and continue until you reach a thatched house at a junction lying
beside a scenic bridge. From here a narrow road leads right for
about 4km to reach the Nire Valley car park.

Time:
About 5 hours.

Map:
OSi Sheet 75.

Suitability:
A challenging outing suitable for fit, well-equipped walkers. In
mist, precise navigation skills are required on the featureless
Comeragh Plateau.

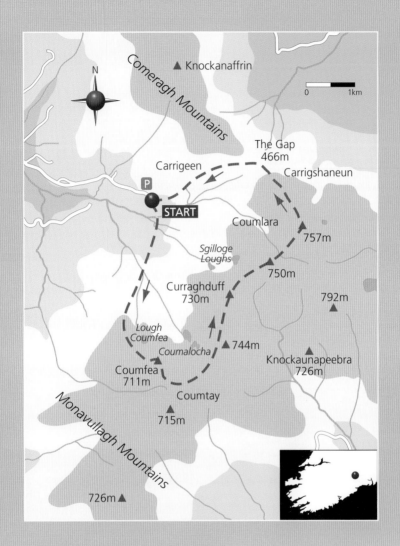

The Nire Valley Coums

Despite the environmental harm created by a decade of largely unregulated economic growth, it is still possible to uncover places where the Celtic Tiger failed to leave a calling card. Waterford's Nire Valley is one example, for this elevated landscape remains rural and appealing, but not in the extravagantly touristy way of pretty footbridges, tea shops, kissing gates and story-boarded viewing points.

Immutable through countless generations, the Nire is instead a jumbled patchwork of sheep pens, small fields, stone walls and improvised fencing – in fact, all the real-life monuments from times when subsistence incomes were hard won from unforgiving mountainsides.

Even today little concession has been made to modernity, and although visitors are welcomed wholeheartedly, it is into a go-as-you-find-it landscape that could double as a film set depicting the unrelenting toil of nineteenth-century upland living.

To begin your exploration of these memorable moorlands, park in the Nire Valley car park **S276 128** (see panel above). Now follow the arrows for the Nire Lakes along a driveway where a sign banning dogs is a reminder that the local economy is heavily dependent on sheep farming.

The Nire Coums

What most walkers do not realise, however, is that these animals also steward the uplands, maintaining biodiversity by controlling the spread of bracken and heather. Any downturn in the viability of upland farming caused by the globalisation of agricultural production should therefore be a concern for hillwalkers. Such a decline would not only endanger the viability of upland communities but also, by removing the benefit of close-grazing sheep, would threaten to transform mountain walking from recreational pleasure to heathery torment.

Next go through a gateway and continue a short distance before swinging left by the rear of a farmhouse to reach another gateway leading to open mountain. A steep descent to the right now leads to a stream in a deep gorge. Cross with care, particularly when water levels are high, before continuing roughly

south, towards a broad spur marking the western extent of the Nire coums.

Every mountain range holds a bank of secrets, and the Comeraghs are no exception. The spur offers a gentle ascent and brings you to a lonesome plateau where the true glory of the area is revealed. Now it is clear that the Comeragh Mountains resemble a huge half-eaten trifle with a series of lake-strewn coums scooped into the massive flanks.

Easy walking and spectacular views now follow on a track above Coumfea and Coumalocha. When the cliff-top route eventually swings east it is worth diverting the short distance south to the rim above Coumtay for a breathtaking vista over a an extravagant tapestry of great cliffs and gullies to the Waterford lowlands and the south coast beyond.

Returning to Coumalocha, you continue contouring the cliff top before heading directly north until you encounter steep ground above the Sgilloge Loughs. Contour right here until you arrive at a stream that topples spectacularly over the cliff top.

When the wind blows directly into this coum it carries spray backwards from the waterfall to form an unmistakable smoke-like plume, which freezes into wonderfully shaped icicles in winter causing local residents to comment that 'the old woman is smoking her pipe again'.

Next head northeast, where a short uphill flog will bring you to the head of Coumlara, a slender coum that, unusually for this area, lacks a lake. Cross the stream at the head of Coumlara and continue until you reach a sturdy fence. Follow this fence left as it descends northwest to reach a steep bouldery rib.

Adrenalin junkies will enjoy the challenge of descending this, but most walkers will be glad to know that this obstacle can be easily bypassed on the left.

Now return to the fence and descend steeply into the Comeragh Gap to reach a stile in the fence where a track marking an ancient Mass path and trade route crosses at right angles to the fence. Follow this route left, which is marked by a series of white poles, as it leads you downhill and then uphill again to reach a gate. From here it is a short but rugged descent to the Nire Valley car park below.

WALK 6
THE MAHON FALLS AND COUMTAY

START:
From Carrick-on-Suir, drive south on the R676 towards
Dungarvan for about 18km. At Mahon Bridge, go right at a
signpost for Mahon Falls and immediately right again beside a
shop. After about 1.5km, turn right and continue through an
entrance with a cattle grid. You are now on the 'magic road'
and the fairy tree is 150m further along on your left.

Time:
Approx. 3½ to 4 hours.

Map:
OSi Sheet 75.

Suitability:
Be aware that this is quite a challenging walk over sometimes
tiring terrain on the elevated and featureless Comeragh
Plateau. As always, be well equipped with warm clothing and
raingear. Carry a map and compass and understand the route
crosses featureless uplands where many have previously
become disorientated when mist descended suddenly.

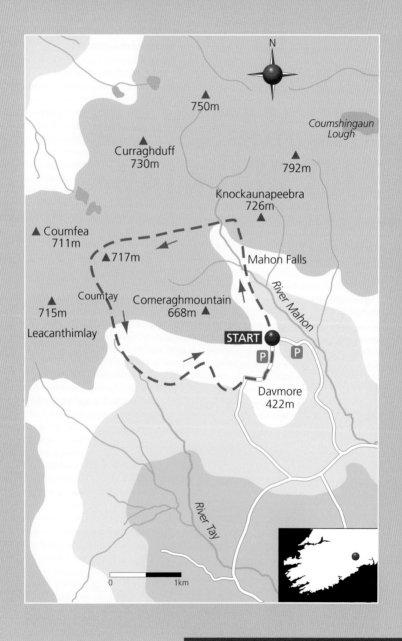

N

750m

Coumshingaun
Lough

Curraghduff
730m

792m

Knockaunapeebra
726m

▲ Coumfea
711m

▲717m

Mahon Falls

River Mahon

Coumtay

Comeraghmountain
668m ▲

715m

Leacanthimlay

START

P   P

Davmore
422m

River Tay

0   1km

The Mahon Falls and Coumtay

A favour-adorned tree beside the 'magic road'

Do you believe the magic went out of life the day you discovered Santa's stocking fillers came, not from Lapland, but more likely from Toyland? If so, never fear, for there still exists in County Waterford a 'magic road' that evokes our earliest experiences of spine-tingling wonder when confronted with something that is resolutely beyond our powers of comprehension.

To relive such evocative moments, follow the road leading to the Mahon Falls in Waterford's Comeragh Mountains (see panel above). At a point just beyond the entrance gate to the Falls and alongside a solitary favour-adorned thorn bush that local tradition claims is a fairy tree, switch off your engine and put your gear shift in neutral. Very soon you will have the disconcerting experience of sitting in a car that is reversing uphill of its own accord.

Dedicated rationalists have visited here with surveying equipment and concluded that the 'magic road' is merely an optical illusion. Most visitors will, however, find it hard to believe this physics-defying piece of magic is merely so when they observe the astonishing speed at which stationary vehicles are propelled upwards.

Still mulling over the improbability of what you have experienced, continue by following the roadway for about 2km into the increasingly timeless Mahon Valley. Stop at a large parking place **S313 080** where at weekends the solitude is invariably hijacked by family groups, picnickers and casual strollers. From here it's 'shank's mare' all the way, starting with a well-trodden footpath leading to the Falls. When this path peters out, cross the River Mahon (with great care when water levels are high) and ascend steep but easy ground, keeping the cascade on your left.

During this ascent you will observe the waters thundering down a 55ft vertical drop into an improbably shallow pool. Amazingly, Tramore canoeist Michael Reynolds kayaked his way down this torrent and survived unhurt to tell the tale. For most people this will come as one more piece of wonder from the Mahon Valley that is scarcely credible without setting eyes on the unquestionably photographic evidence. From the top of the Falls, continue ascending until it is safe to recross the Mahon River.

Now in welcome solitude, strike out west over the heathery Comeragh Plateau for about 1.5km of gently rising ground. Here the going can be somewhat tedious and you will be forced to climb with regularity into the bed of some (hopefully) dry watercourses. Your efforts are well rewarded, however, when you reach the cliffs of Coumfea and experience the breathtaking vista from above this lake-strewn corrie that gazes out over the majestic tablecloth of the renowned Nire Valley.

Now head in a southerly direction from Coumfea and continue until your way is barred by the complex architecture of the great cliffs above Coumtay. Here the view is southwards but no less majestic and includes the Waterford coast, Dungarvan Harbour and Helvick Head.

Do not attempt to descend directly into Coumtay as much of the south- and east-facing cliff is sheer and punctuated by treacherous gullies. Instead, move left until the angle of slope eases and it is possible to descend safely into the eastern side of the Coum. Now follow downhill from the outfall of the River Tay until you are beside a ruined farmhouse secluded in a clump of trees.

Take the track leading uphill and go left from here to a gate. Then skirt the side of a forest on a rougher track that leads to a tarmacadam roadway. Follow this left and uphill to your parking place, which is just out of sight beyond the highest point of the roadway.

WALK 7
COUMSHINGAUN AND CROTTY'S LOUGH

START:

Kilclooney Wood car park is located in County Waterford beside the R676 and close to the midpoint between Carrick-on-Suir and Dungarvan.

Time:

Allow about 5 hours to complete the longer route visiting Fauscoum and Crotty's Rock. The circuit of Coumshingaun should take about 3½ to 4 hours to complete.

Map:

OSi Sheet 75.

Suitability:

Even in good weather this is a demanding outing. Carry a map and compass and on the longer walk have at least one person in the group who is competent to navigate on the featureless Comeragh Plateau.

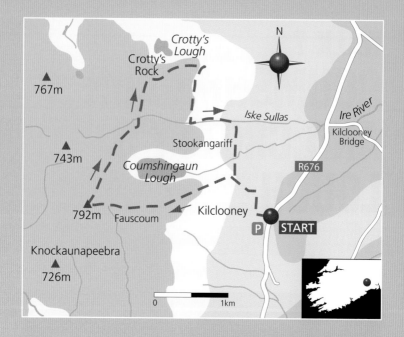

Crotty's
Lough

Crotty's
Rock

▲
767m

N

Iske Sullas

Ire River

Kilclooney
Bridge

Stookangariff

▲
743m

Coumshingaun
Lough

R676

792m   Fauscoum

Kilclooney

P   START

Knockaunapeebra
▲
726m

0   1km

Coumshingaun and Crotty's Lough

Someone or some body owns all the land of Ireland and, unlike in many other countries, we don't have a legal right to roam. So with legislative uncertainty you might expect access problems to abound and, indeed, for a time about a decade ago such issues threatened to close large tracts of the Irish countryside.

This did not happen for, in the main, people respond positively to incentive. And these days many landowners are gaining merited reward from countryside recreation through admirable initiatives such as the Walks Scheme and the Rural Social Scheme. As a result landowners are mostly welcoming to hillwalkers, with access problems hugely diminished and eventually perhaps becoming as uncommon as poverty-stricken politicians. For the moment, however, a number of flashpoints still remain with Sod's Law dictating they almost inevitably occur at scenically compelling locations.

One example is Crotty's Lough in the Comeragh Mountains. This achingly beautiful coum comes complete with an epic saga of dispossessed natives taking to the hills in tempestuous times to wage war on wealthy intruders. Every epic needs a hero, of course, and in this case it is in the form of outlaw William Crotty who – as you probably already suspect – robbed the rich to help the poor, until finally betrayed by a companion and executed in 1742.

For several years Crotty's Lough has been closed for public access but it is still possible to view – if not actually visit – this evocative amphitheatre from one of Ireland's finest hillwalks starting from Kilclooney Wood car park **S340 102** (see panel above).

Begin by taking a sylvan track (west) to join a forestry road. Then follow this roadway (right) past a disguised deflector mast until it crosses a fence to open mountainside. Now it is upwards through scrubby terrain towards a prominent boulder on the skyline. Here you will clearly see your objective, the ridgeline rising to the left of Coumshingaun. This may seem intimidating and, indeed, it can be a lung-burning challenge, but the rocky scrambling on this arête is actually both easy and enjoyable. All you require is sufficient bottle for the shortish battle until the slope eases above majestic Coumshingaun – the largest lake in the Comeragh Mountains and the finest example of a corrie lake on these islands.

Now it is pleasantly elevated walking above great gullies that dive abruptly to the brooding waters far below until one final steepening bars your route. This is the Becher's Brook of your walk and should be taken with care, particularly in wet or icy conditions. Once above this hurdle, however, you are safely on the great vastness of the Comeragh Plateau and are now at liberty to choose your own horizon.

If you lack confidence in navigation, it is best simply to circumnavigate the coum, keeping the lake to you right. Do a full 360 degrees and you will eventually rejoin your original route up from Kilclooney.

Otherwise, strike out bravely across featureless moorland towards the small cairn that marks point 792m, the highest top in the Comeraghs. Commonly this is referred to as Fauscoum but on the OSi map Fauscoum actually denotes the lakeless corrie directly south of Coumshingaun – so confusion reigns. Whatever its proper title, one thing is certain: this is a grand place to tarry and banquet on superb views over the West Comeraghs, the Knockmealdown Mountains, the Waterford lowlands and the distant sparkle of the Atlantic Ocean.

Next go northeast to pick up the precipice west of Coumshingaun and follow its edge until it swings sharply east. Here you instead strike out almost due north for about 500m to reach a cliff top that offers a tantalising window on the inaccessible tranquillity of Crotty's Lough laid out below. Follow the cliffs (right) to the prominent pinnacle known as Crotty's Rock for a marvellous vista. This was once the outlaw's lookout point and on the other end of the lake – and unfortunately barred to walkers at the time of writing – lies the claustrophobic but otherwise accessible cave that was his refuge. After Crotty's execution his wife is reputed to have thrown herself to her death from these rocks, which still bear the outlaw's name.

To return, head directly south until you encounter Iske Sullas ('the water of light'). Keeping the stream to your right – but not too closely as there are sharp drops – descend until the slope eases below a final waterfall. Now traverse right to cross Iske Sullas and the moraines at the mouth of Coumshingaun. These will lead you to a path that ascends to the large boulder encountered earlier. From here it is a short ramble down to Kilclooney.

Coumshingaun Lough

WALK 8
THE CIRCUIT OF GLENARY

START:
About 2km from Clonmel on the R 671 Clonmel/Dungarvan road and just beyond a row of houses, take a minor road left. Continue uphill until Carey's Castle car park and picnic site are signed to your left. Your walk begins here.

Time:
3 hours.

Map:
OSi Sheets 74 and 75.

Suitability:
Generally an unchallenging outing ideal for those with moderate fitness. In mist some navigation skills are required. Note: when water levels are high in the Glenary stream it is inadvisable to cross at Carey's Castle. Instead continue west to a public road and then a right turn leads to a bridge where you go straight ahead on a wide forest trail leading back to your parking place.

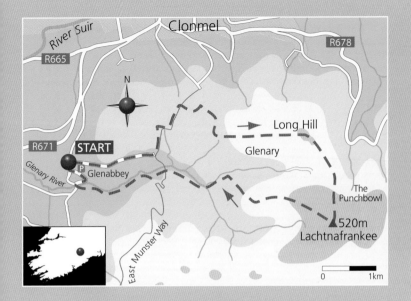

The Circuit of Glenary

Deep in the Comeragh Mountains above Clonmel there exists a mock-Tudor mansion, a hillside farmhouse, an obtrusively unblended religious cross and a firing range. Now you may be wondering how the developers got away with such blatant intrusions on the mountain environment. The answer is simple: they didn't apply for planning permission.

Surely time, then, for righteous indignation, references to brown envelopes and calls for the removal of these monstrosities? Actually, no! You see, most of the structures in Waterford's Glenary Valley are from a time when planning requirements were unheard of. The mansion is the eighteenth-century Carey's Castle and it was once actually due for demolition after falling into dangerous disrepair, but locals protested and so it was secured and preserved.

Would Glenary be better if some forgotten planning law had maintained it, pristine and unaltered, by human hand? Probably not. Carey's Castle tells the story of a short-lived and misguided struggle to tame the uplands. And the deserted hillside farmhouse tells of a longer battle lost. Indeed, the drystone walls, the bridle paths and field systems of Glenary seem not so much as incongruous intrusions as monuments to the endeavour of previous generations. For Glenary is actually a green museum to a departed era and for this reason alone it is well worth a visit.

Looking out from the Holy Year Cross above Clonmel to a snow-capped Slievenamon

To enjoy an outing that punches well above its weight in terms of variety and scenery, begin at Carey's Castle car park **S186 191** (see panel above). From here return to the public road, go right and immediately right again. Follow the Munster Way signs to the end of a minor road and then left and uphill on an increasingly muddy track. When open mountainside appears to the right leave the track and head over rough ground to a stile over a wire fence. Now part from the walking arrows and ascend east until the going levels and an altar site and Holy Year Cross appear ahead. Here there are superb views over Clonmel to Slievenamon and each year on an August Monday, the faithful labour uphill in throngs for a celebration of Mass.

Next descend southeast on a broad track. On your right you will pass the abandoned farmstead of the Ireland family. The Irelands have long since given up the unequal struggle with the hillside and the result is that the forces of nature are now busy reclaiming their once-productive fields.

Reflecting, perhaps, on how mountains ultimately defeat all human endeavour, continue uphill to the cairned summit of Long Hill and then veer south as the route drops to a coll. Located above a wooded amphitheatre known as the Punchbowl, this makes an ideal lunch stop.

Refreshed, you now tackle the steepest pull of the day that draws you upwards to Laghtnafrankee summit (520m). The effort is worth it, for this is an exceptional viewing point offering a full 360-degree vista of the Comeragh, Galtee and Knockmealdown Mountains. Leave the summit by a wide shoulder running roughly west. This descent can be tedious but soon you reach the valley and join a track above the busy Glenary River. Cross a tributary of the Glenary – with some difficulty when water levels are high – and continue over a fence and into a wood where a narrow path rapidly leads to a forest roadway.

Across the river to your right there exists a field system and some overgrown ruins. This is all that remains of the once-flourishing village of Glenary, which in the nineteenth century had a population of over 200 and remained an Irish-speaking community into the twentieth century. Unable to maintain its population in more affluent times it was finally abandoned in the early 1960s.

Continuing generally west along the forest roadway while keeping the river below on the right, you will, by watching carefully, observe through the trees a ruined building on the opposite bank. Cross the Glenary to visit the once-proud Carey's Castle, built at the beginning of the nineteenth century on the site of an earlier monastery by a newly prosperous school-owning family from Clonmel but abandoned less than half century later. From here a track leads an easy 500m through pleasant mixed woodland to your parking place.

Carey's Castle

*The Munster Way as it
traverses above Glenary*

WALK 9
KNOCKANAFFRIN RIDGE

START:
From Clonmel follow the R678 for Rathgormuck and Portlaw. About 2km beyond Harney's Cross, the main road swings sharply left but go straight ahead on a wide gravel track to reach a small parking place at **S285 180**. This marks the start of the Mohra Loop walk and here a map board outlines the route to Lough Mohra.

Time:
Approx. 4 hours.

Map:
OSi Sheet 75.

Suitability:
Moderately challenging outing suitable for well-equipped walkers with reasonable fitness. In mist, navigation skills are required on the trackless section of the walk.

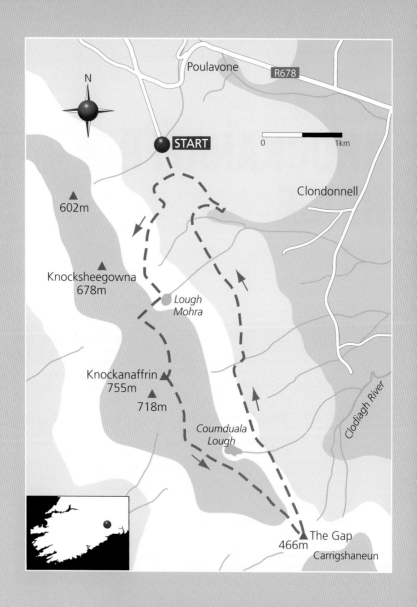

Poulavone

R678

Clondonnell

START

N

602m

Knocksheegowna
678m

Lough
Mohra

Knockanaffrin
755m

718m

Coumduala
Lough

Clodiagh River

The Gap
466m

Carrigshaneun

0   1km

Knockanaffrin Ridge

The slopes of the Knockanaffrin Ridge looking towards Knocksheegowna

The Comeragh Mountains always remind me a little of a giant butterfly with the east wing formed by the great Comeragh Plateau and its surrounding necklace of steep cliffs and wonderfully glaciated coums. The west wing is fashioned by the unassuming hills above Glenary that offer a not hugely demanding circuit with plenty of interest along the way. Finally, the slender Knockanaffrin Ridge provides the delicate unifying spine of the Comeraghs. Appropriately this fine ridge also offers a five-star walking experience that is a foretaste of greater ruggedness to come on the memorable ridges of Ireland's southwest.

To complete the Knockanaffrin Ridge, park above Glenpatrick and beside the blocked-off entrance road to a ruined scout's hut (see panel above). Knockanaffrin now dominates the skyline above and from this angle it comes across as one of our shapeliest natural beauties and always reminds me of Croagh Patrick, which is surely Ireland's handsomest hill. Now follow the red arrows of the Lough Mohra Loop upwards before branching right on the spur walk to lonely Lough Mohra.

Next walk up the moraines above on a short but steepish ascent to the Knockanaffrin Ridge proper. You are now standing on the col between Knocksheegowna and Knockanaffrin and on a clear day will be enjoying great views over the captivating Nire Valley to the Waterford coastline beyond.

Next swing left and head up towards the 755m summit of Knockanaffrin ('the Mass mountain'), a symmetrical pyramid that comes with plenty of historic echoes from penal times when Mass was celebrated in remote places far removed from the prying eyes of officialdom. The ridge hereabouts is actually an unlikely place of worship since it consists of a series of rocky tors – known locally as the Seven Sisters – which now provide you with invigorating but easy scrambling opportunities until you reach the prominent boulder point that marks the high point of the ridge.

Eventually, a short descent accompanied by immense views into the jaws of the Nire coums brings you over a fence to a levelling of the ridge above Coumduala Lough. Those with silky scrambling skills can 'adrenalinise' the outing at this stage by descending an appealing gully to directly access this pretty tarn below, but those wishing to appreciate the ridge in its entirety should continue onwards through a marvellously unspoilt landscape to pick up a fence that canters straight downhill to the Comeragh Gap. Here white poles mark an ancient trade pathway that has now become a pleasant walkway, but this is not your route. Swing sharply left instead and begin contouring northwest beneath the crags of the Knockanaffrin Ridge.

You are now traversing trackless mountainside but the going should be pleasant enough as you continue below Coumduala and head towards a forest. The exact location point of the path you are seeking can be difficult to identify and so it is best to aim off by staying on a relatively high contour and then descend with a fence on your left until the forest track becomes plainly visible.

Cross a fence to join this track as it meanders pleasantly through forest and open countryside with great views over the Suir Valley to Slievenamon and beyond. Eventually swing left at a T–Junction and continue past a barrier to your parking place while reflecting, perhaps, that the Knockanaffrin Ridge is hard to beat for high scenic reward as a return on modest effort.

Lough Mohra with Knockanaffrin rising above

WALK 10
COUM IARTHAR

START:
From Clonmel follow the R678 for Rathgormuck to Clondonnell Crossroads at S312 183, which bears a sign for the Boolas and the Gap. Go right here and drive a further 3km going straight ahead through two intersections and eventually following a boreen to park in Curraheen farmyard.

Time:
Approx. 4 to 5 hours.

Map:
OSi Sheet 75.

Suitability:
Challenging outing suitable for well-equipped walkers with fitness and some head for heights.

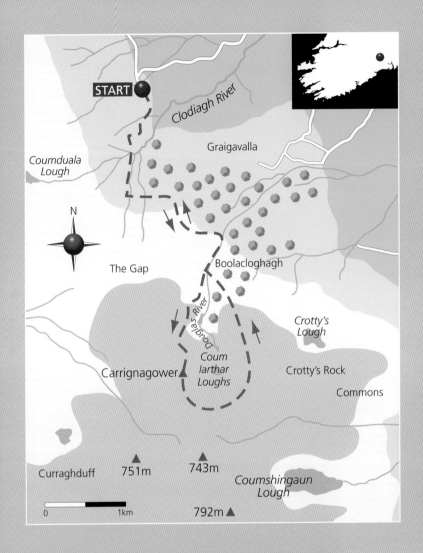

START

Clodiagh River

Coumduala
Lough

Graigavalla

N

The Gap

Boolacloghagh

Douglas River

Crotty's
Lough

Coum
Iarthar
Loughs

Carrignagower

Crotty's Rock

Commons

Curraghduff

751m

743m

Coumshingaun
Lough

0   1km

792m

The Curraheen Trailhead heading towards Coum
Iarthar, known locally as 'the Boolas'.

Problems with access rarely occur high in the Irish mountains; instead they are more likely to happen at upland access points. For a long time the north side of the Comeragh Mountains was such an area. This fertile plateau came with access problems at Crotty's Lough and a pattern of intensive agriculture and small fields that, understandably, made entrance to the hills most problematic. And this was unfortunate, for one of the gems of the Comeragh Mountains is tucked away in this area.

Coum Iarthar – known locally as 'the Boolas' – is a compelling but little-visited corrie, mainly because, up to now, the principal route of access has been from the Nire Valley, which lies well to the west on the other side of the Comeragh Gap. Recession is, however, often the father of ingenuity and so in recent times there has been a greater emphasis placed on making the Irish countryside more accessible for tourists.

Fáilte Ireland has developed a series of themed looped walks that can be completed in half a day or less, which return users conveniently to their starting point. One such trail in the Waterford countryside not only provides a lovely outing in itself but has also greatly improved access to the Boola lakes and the plateau above Coum Iarthar.

The Curraheen Trail heading towards Coum Iarthar, known locally as 'the Boolas'.

To explore the north side of the east Comeraghs, start from the Curraheen Trailhead, **S306 153**, which is located in an old farmyard built in the Irish vernacular style of having the farm outbuildings in a courtyard to the front of the farmhouse. Then follow the walking arrows along an enclosed rural lane before turning right and passing over a stile into a field. Continue following the arrows through a series of small fields and past a map-board to reach open mountainside.

Here a spur walk is signed (right) for Coumduala Lough but you continue ahead with Crotty's Rock – known locally as 'the ass's ears' – protruding above the skyline as if a huge donkey was resting in the next valley. Cross several streams with convenient footbridges to reach the corner of Graigavalla forest. Keeping the trees on your left, pass a large rock on your right and continue to reach the infant Douglas River flowing at right angles to your route. Here, a line of white poles marks an ancient trade route across the Comeraghs, known locally as 'Bóithrín na Sochraide' since it was also used to carry coffins from the upper Nire Valley to Rathgormuck Church.

Your objective, however, lies uphill. With the stream on your left, ascend into the impressive jaws of Coum larthar. Keep to the right-hand side of the coum and you will notice a great blade of rock that stands out from the cliff wall. Ascend steep ground now to reach a small grassy col directly inside this rock blade while admiring the wonderfully complex architecture of the coum wall immediately on your right. You may now notice that this rock pinnacle bears a distinct resemblance to Scotland's famous inaccessible pinnacle in the Cuillin Hills of Skye. About 100m long and 15m high, it is the only non-coastal Irish top I know that requires rock climbing of, at least, very difficult standard to ascend even by its easiest route.

Unless you are a confident rock climber, do not be lured into attempting an ascent of the pinnacle. Instead this is a good place to settle and enjoy lunch, particularly on a sunny day.

Afterwards, continue by descending slightly and then swinging sharply right to scramble up a disrupted gully followed by steep but more open ground to reach the Comeragh Plateau. From here it is possible to go directly ahead and soon encounter a fence that can be followed right all the way down to the head of the Comeragh Gap from where walking arrows will lead you all the way back to the Curraheen Trailhead. However, this can be an unpleasant knee-jarring descent, where non-scramblers must be careful to bypass (on the left) a steep rocky down-climb.

A much better option is to go counterclockwise instead and circuit the corrie above its four picturesque paternoster lakes with the almost circular innermost Boola constituting the highest lake in the Comeraghs. Continue all the way around the coum and then descend on reasonably pleasant terrain to reach the floor of the coum beside the outermost lake. Now it is a question of retracing your steps by following the yellow arrows back to the Curraheen Trailhead.

View from the Boola Pinnacle towards the
east-facing cliffs of Coum Iarthar

The unusual kidney-shaped inner lake at Muskry taken from near O'Loughlin's Castle.

THE GALTEE MOUNTAINS

From the M8 south of Cashel the great rampart of the Galtee Mountain range rises abruptly and seems to bar the way south implacably with no chink in its mighty armour. Unlike the Knockmealdowns and Comeraghs, the Galtees consist of an unbroken east/west rampart interspersed by conical peaks with no roads splitting the range. Indeed Ireland's highest inland mountains formed an exasperating barrier to early railway builders and forced the Dublin–Cork railway to loop into south Limerick and north Cork while the new M8 motorway bypasses to the east.

To explore these high mountains it is necessary to forgo the world of motorised transport and travel exclusively on foot. This is made easier by the fact that, for the most part, the Galtees are cloaked by blanket bog and present a reasonably benign aspect to the walker approaching from the south. The north side of the range is also easily accessible but startlingly different with a much more untamed grandeur. The jewels of the Galtees are secreted here – great steep-sided corries that eat into the mountainside to hold five austerely enchanting lakes beneath the shadow of the main Galty Ridge.

WALK 11
THE CIRCUIT OF GLENCUSHNABINNA

START:
From Lisvernane village, in Aherlow, go east along the R663 towards Bansha. After a kilometre turn right and then go left at a T-junction. A short distance beyond is Clydagh Bridge, and soon after the fingerpost for Galtymore points right. After about 300m, park at the forest entrance on the right.

Time:
5 hours.

Map:
OSi Sheet 74.

Suitability:
Be in no doubt that this is a challenging walk requiring good fitness and reaching considerable altitude. Be fully kitted out with spare clothing and raingear. Carry a map and compass and be aware that around Galtymore summit walkers become disorientated in mist with monotonous regularity.

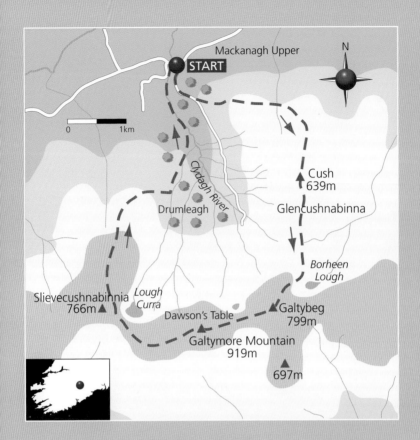

The Circuit of Glencushnabinna

It is sometimes said that work is the curse of the drinking classes. This may or may not be true but one thing is certain, employment commitments are a continual thorn in the side of those yearning for the freedom of the hills. So many wonderful walks begging footfall and so few leave days to complete them! This tyranny of choice means that for most people it is a question of being selective with walks. If this applies to you and you can find time for only one outing in County Tipperary, then it must be the circuit of Glencushnabinna. This high-level loop ticks all the right boxes as it passes over the elegant tops of three outstanding summits including Galtymore where on a crystal-clear day Carrauntoohil and Lugnaquilla are at once in view.

For a great day on the hills park at Clydagh Bridge **R874 278** (see panel above). Then follow the minor road south into Glencushnabinna (spelt

View of Galtymore from Glencushnabinna

'Glencoshnabinnia' on the OSi map) past another car park before climbing steps to a stile (left) and taking a path upwards. Initially the ascent toils through heathery fields before rising over open mountainside to Cush (639m), the first top of your circuit.

Marketing gurus generally hold that the three factors determining consumer demand are location, location and location. If so, this fine peak is simply in the wrong place to attract substantial footfall. For if Cush were transported to the Slieve Bloom or Cooley Mountains it would instantly become a renowned five-star ridge, raising its shoulders imperiously above the surrounding summits and acting as an irresistible honeypot for walkers.

Being a mere outlier to the higher Galtee peaks comes with the advantage, however, of remaining delightfully less visited. So, most likely enjoying your own company, proceed along the wonderfully airy Cush Ridge.

The teardrop-shaped Borheen Lough

Soon after, you descend to a scenic col, from where the next ascent is a two-stage thigh-burner. The effort proves worthwhile, however, when you sashay easily above the perfect teardrop shape of Borheen Lough before swinging right along the Galtybeg Ridge. And then comes your 'wow' moment: enormous views open suddenly south to the Knockmealdown and Comeragh Mountains while north you gaze over pastoral Aherlow to Slievenamuck and the Slievefelim Hills.

The short descent from Galtybeg leads to a col, made muddy by the growing popularity of the easier south route to Ireland's only inland 3,000ft peak. From here the ascent of Galtymore may not rate as a true thigh-burner, but it is a conversation killer, and you will doubtless be glad to reach the flat-topped summit (919m) knowing the day's hardest work is now behind.

Here you are far less likely to find solitude, but your eyes will immediately be drawn to a white Celtic cross overlooking Aherlow, which was painstakingly erected by Tipperary man Ted Kavanagh in 1975. It is actually the fourth cross to be erected on the summit during the last century and its pristine condition is accounted for by local hillwalker and mountain rescuer Jimmy Barry, who for the past decade has taken upon himself the task of painting this cross annually.

Leaving the cross in your slipstream, head west along the summit plateau to a large cairn before descending towards an area of black bog where you pick up the Galty Wall. This impressive drystone structure was built in the late nineteenth century to divide two landholdings and still runs 3,500m along the Galty Ridge. Follow this wall as it traverses delicately above Lough Curra before parting company with it when it swings left.

Your route now continues generally north on a broad spur descending towards Glencushnabinna. Aim for a marker post on a raised knoll below and to your right, from where a line of poles leads to a stile entering Drumleagh Wood. Once in woodland just follow the meandering arrows for about 2km through sylvan surroundings as they lead you pleasantly back to your starting place.

WALK 12
WEST GALTEES

START:
Leave the M8 Portlaoise–Cork motorway at junction 12 and follow the signs for Kilbeheny village. Go through the village and continue a short distance beyond on the old N8. Then turn left at a sign for King's Yard and follow this road straight uphill past a water-treatment works. Immediately afterwards stop at a Y-junction, where there are limited parking opportunities. Your walk now takes the uphill lane directly ahead.

Time:
5 hours.

Map:
OSi Sheet 74.

Suitability:
Although the going never gets terribly tough, this is a challenging walk that reaches considerable altitude. So be well kitted out with warm clothing and raingear. Carry a map and compass and be aware that the route, apart from the Galty Wall section offers few navigational handrails.

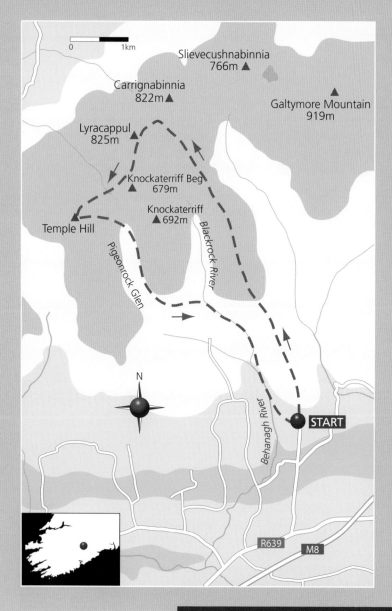

Slievecushnabinnia
766m ▲

Carrignabinnia
822m▲

Galtymore Mountain
919m

Lyracappul
825m
▲

Knockaterriff Beg
679m
▲

Knockaterriff
▲692m

Temple Hill

Pigeonrock Glen

Blackrock River

Behanagh River

N

START

R639   M8

West Galtees

Whenever I return to the West Galtees I immediately feel I have been away too long, for the outline of these insouciant hills immediately weaves a spell. The narrow pastoral valleys, drystone walls and rounded tops instantly recall, as they always have, strong resonances of the Lakeland dales and fells.

There was a time when I was a relentless cheerleader for these unfrequented uplands, but then I drifted away, seduced by sexier ranges with compelling gullies, rocky ridges and ice-crusted summits. But sooner or later I always return, for these hills beckon the rambler who wishes to leave the world of branded convenience and mechanised transport for the experience of true solitude in a timeless landscape.

To explore these little-frequented uplands, amble straight ahead up the lane from your parking place at **R869 197** (see panel above) towards the great whaleback of Monabrack Mountain. After following the laneway to its end swing right, past a deserted farmhouse enclosed by a stand of trees and head out onto rough pastureland along a broad crest that heads just west of north.

Eventually, the crest narrows and you reach the cairned summit of Monabrack (629m), which offers one of the most striking views at the heart of the Galtees. There are mountains in all directions from Galtymore to Temple Hill and Lyracappul to Knockaterriff.

So far so wonderfully scenic, but now you are faced with an inconveniently steep loss of height to a col below the Galty Ridge. From here you have the option to follow downhill along a switchback track that was used to draw turf from the mountain in a less-affluent era.

The track leads into the Blackrock Valley and eventually back to the walk start point, by way of the eastern slopes of Knockaterriff, but true mountaineers will be unable to resist the heart-thumping ascent that toils steeply up a spur to the Galty Wall. There they will find that this impressive drystone structure, built in the late nineteenth century to divide two great estates, is a most useful navigational aid if weather conditions are poor.

Whenever I encounter mountaintop structures such as the Galty Wall, I cannot help but wonder about the builders. Did they walk up each day from the valley, irrespective of weather? What kind of protective clothing did they have in harsh conditions? Did they ever get lost or have an accident on their descent? We will never know for sure, but one thing is certain, these teak-tough individuals created an enduring structure that, for over a century, has survived the harshest Galtee storms.

Magnificent views now unfold into the Glen of Aherlow as you follow the wall (left) to the tiny cairn at Lyracappul ('Confluence of the Horse'). This small eminence from the ridge improbably represents the highest mountain entirely in County Limerick and the second-highest point in the Galtees.

After Lyrracappul your next objective is Temple Hill – the most westerly of the major mountains in the Galtee range. It is inadvisable to take the direct route, however. Instead, keep on the highest ground as you descend along a broad ridge towards Knockaterriff Beg, being careful to stay above the great gullies that cut away to the right to the Glen of Aherlow far below.

Do not continue all the way to Knockaterriff Beg summit but instead descend to a col and then ascend steeply to reach the shapely summit of Temple Hill, which is crowned by a great unexcavated burial cairn. These cairns are a

Looking towards Knockaterriff in January snows

feature of many Irish mountaintops and great efforts were clearly made to mark the resting place of some now forgotten personages since such cairns are clearly designed to be visible from the surrounding lowlands.

This is your final major objective for the day and in clear conditions it is a place to tarry and enjoy the wonderful view across the fertile heartland of the Golden Vale to the distant shimmering outline of the Cork and Kerry hills beyond. Next, head downhill for a confluence of streams that marks the start of the Pigeonrock River valley.

Here is a serenely sheltered place to take lunch, as it is almost totally devoid of distant views and perfectly meets the requirement for oneness with nature. After your repast, leave with reluctance and ramble along the riverbank, as the valley grows wider. Eventually you will pass through double gates beside a new farm building near where the Pigeonrock and Blackrock streams coalesce to form the Behanagh River.

For some unknown reason, no less a personage than the Elizabethan poet Edmund Spenser – who resided at Kilcolman Castle, County Cork – chanced this way and expressed himself enthralled by this meeting of waters. Continue following a rough road south as the Behanagh gurgles happily alongside.

Next pass through a gate and then join with another lane before saying a last goodbye to the Behanagh and following this minor road to a junction near a waterworks. Turn left and soon afterwards you are back at your parking place. As you drive away, you will most likely vow not to be tardy with your next visit to the sublime west Galtees.

WALK 13
THE CIRCUIT OF LOUGH MUSKRY

START:
Take the N24 Waterford–Limerick road to Bansha village. Then follow signs for the Glen of Aherlow, but very soon take a left at a sign for Rossadrehid. At Rossadrehid, cross a main road to a minor road that eventually swings right. Soon after, park at an island of trees by a forest entrance.

Time:
2½ hours for the out-and-back walk to Lough Muskry. Allow 4 hours for the Galty Ridge section.

Map:
OSi Sheet 74.

Suitability:
The walk into Lake Muskry follows a waymarked track all the way. There are a few steepish sections, but generally this walk is suitable for family groups and strollers. If you venture on to Galty Ridge, however, you should be well equipped and have the navigational skills required for high-altitude walking.

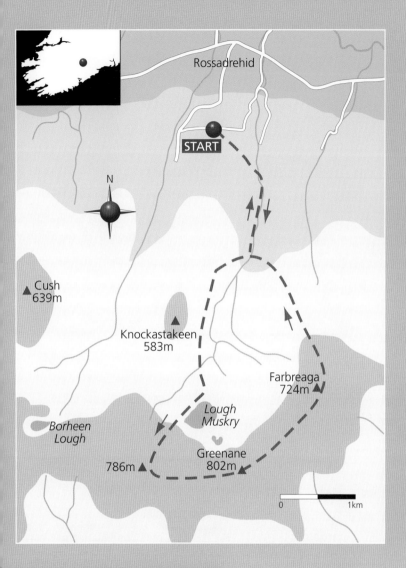

Rossadrehid

START

N

Cush
639m

Knockastakeen
583m

Farbreaga
724m ▲

Lough
Muskry

Borheen
Lough

Greenane
786m ▲   802m ▲

0   1km

The Circuit of Lough Muskry

There was a time when you could spend an entire day traversing many of our best-known trails and not meet another soul. Recently, however, our trekking routes have become less neglected with overseas walker numbers increasing rapidly and Irish people also recognising the breezy self-improvement that comes with outdoor exercising.

Of course, the number of trail users is not yet comparable to the Camino or Scotland's Highland Way, but there is still no doubt that the Irish countryside is increasingly becoming the playground of walkers. Economic downturns typically make us time rich but cash poor and in such circumstances we quickly discover that walking offers healthy and costless recreation.

So if chance encounters are not your bag, you may now resign yourself to less solitary rambles such as the west Galtees and west Knockmealdowns. But if you believe that hikes are enriched by an occasional chat the busy path to Lough Muskry is just the place for you.

To begin your walk follow the indispensable walking arrows placed by the industrious Aherlow Fáilte Society that start at **R917 283** and lead up through a forested area before trending right and more steeply uphill to a stile at a gate leading to open moorland.

From here the track, which was originally built to facilitate the extraction of water from Lough Muskry, roughens and steepens. In some ways, it is an intrusive scar on an otherwise pristine landscape, but it also provides a convenient handrail deep into the heart of the Galtees for casual ramblers and is, on balance, a good thing.

Now the moorland track undulates pleasantly with the brooding gullies of the dark Muskry cliffs drawing ever closer. One more sharpish pull and you are beside the lake that local legend holds was once the abode of a slew of pretty damsels who on alternate years were transformed into birds.

It is almost obligatory for walkers to stop by the lakeside but eventually a decision must be made. If a short outing was your objective then simply retrace your steps from here and follow the walking arrows back to your start point.

If you wish to continue, however, you should now get upwardly mobile on the high moraines west of the lough and continue

Walkers traversing the moraines above Lough Muskry

towards the slopes that rise invitingly to the right of the great cliffs and offer an easy gateway to the Galty Ridge. Head up the grassy slopes and then swing left towards the curious outcrop of O'Loughlin's Castle that sits astride the Galty Ridge proper. From a distance this unusual edifice resembles a man-made construction, but it is actually a natural phenomenon created by frost-shattered rock dating from the time in the Ice Age when only the mountaintops protruded above the ice sheets. You will find, however, that today it offers memorable views past the Knockmealdown Mountains to the south coast.

Once you forsake the solitude of O'Loughlin's Castle keep the cliffs to your left while ascending Greenane (802m) and then continue northeast along the broad crest to a ruined building on the summit of Farbreaga that was probably a booley, which served as a shelter for farmers tending upland flocks.

Here the main Galty Ridge dog-legs sharply right, but the route back to your start point goes roughly northwest and begins descending a sometimes tedious spur that is, however, enlivened by views towards Galtymore and Galtybeg that show both mountains to their very best advantage.

Eventually, after crossing a stream as it enters a wood, which must be approached with great care when water levels are high, you continue uphill to reach the stile by a gate that earlier allowed access to the open mountainside. Now just retrace your steps following the convenient directional arrows to the walk start point.

WALK 14
GALTYMORE FROM THE BLACK ROAD

START:
Leave the M8 Portlaoise–Cork motorway at Junction 11 and take the old N8 south towards Mitchelstown. Near a derelict house just north of Skeheenarinky village a fingerpost for 'Galtymore climb' points right to a minor road. Follow this road for 3km to its end. Park in the small car park here.

Time:
3½ hours.

Map:
OSi Sheet 74.

Suitability:
This is a challenging walk to a high summit that is often very windy and extremely cold so be equipped with warm clothing and raingear. Return from the end of the Black Road if unsure of the route. Use a map and compass and be aware that the second half of the route crosses open mountainside where it is easy to become disorientated in poor visibility.

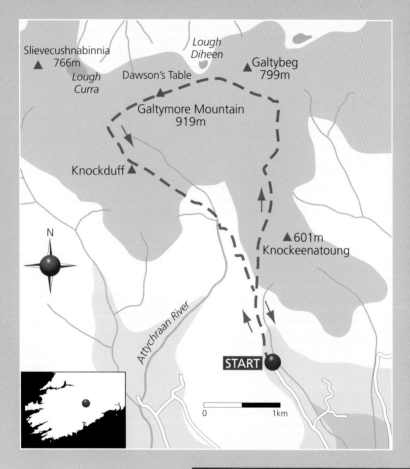

Slievecushnabinnia
▲ 766m

Lough
Curra

Lough
Diheen

Dawson's Table

Galtybeg
▲ 799m

Galtymore Mountain
919m

Knockduff ▲

N

▲601m
Knockeenatoung

Attychraan River

START

0   1km

Galtymore from the Black Road

Most readers will be surprised to learn that this Irish mountain resonates with romantic associations for many couples. For well over half a century the landmark London dancehall bearing the name of Ireland's highest inland mountain spawned countless dalliances and an abundance of lifelong partnerships. Until it finally closed in 2009, the Galtymore in Cricklewood acted as a social club, home from home and gateway to love for generations of Irish emigrants.

You are, of course, less likely to discover lifelong romance on the eponymous County Tipperary mountain – although you never know – but what you will certainly come upon is a fine, airy circuit with magnificent views as a reward for relatively modest investment of time and effort.

From your parking place at **R893 203** (see panel above) follow the laneway leading through two gates to a track on open mountainside. This is the Black

*The monument to the four men who died
in the 1976 Galtee aircrash*

The south side of Galtymore and the Galty Ridge pictured from Knockeenatoung

The O'Reilly family from Thurles enjoy a perfect summer day on Galtymore summit. (Courtesy C. Needham)

Road, an old route previously used to draw turf from the mountain, but now a convenient high-level entry point to the heart of the Galtees.

After about 20 minutes of gentle ascent you will observe a stone monument in the shape of an aircraft tail about 50m to your right. It was erected to the memory of four Abbeyshrule airmen who died in a crash on a nearby mountainside in September 1976. This tragic event triggered the foundation, in 1977, of the South Eastern Mountain Rescue Association, which now provides a comprehensive rescue service across several mountain ranges.

The going now steepens, and the Black Road swings right and then left before petering out in the shadow of Galtybeg Mountain. From this point head onto the lower slopes of Galtybeg, then head left for the col with Galtymore.

Here the countless footfalls over the years have rendered the peat hags muddy and unpleasant, but the compensation is a splendid view over the renowned Glen of Aherlow and a more immediate vista into the unusual, vat-like Lough Diheen, lying 200m beneath your feet and reputed to be the home of a serpent. If you decide to linger in the hope of a photo opportunity, however, you should prepare for a long wait. Local legend holds that the shy serpent in the murky depths surfaces but once in seven years.

When the inveterate traveller Robert Lloyd Praeger came this way, he did not encounter the serpent but did remark on the 'savage grandeur' and lifeless gloom of Diheen. You may wish to reflect on the insightful accuracy of this observation as you now go left and (carefully) ascend the cliffs towards Galtymore summit.

On reaching the top many people are surprised to discover that this is not exclusively a County Tipperary mountain and that they have also reached the highest point of County Limerick. Galtymore's two-county, twin-cairned top consists of a surprisingly flat plateau that is mostly cold and inhospitable. The altitude and inland location mean that in winter it regularly holds snow, and it is not uncommon to encounter, during a cold snap, winter-sports enthusiasts tobogganing or snowboarding on the mountains steep flanks.

Beyond the summit (919m), the plateau bears an iron Celtic cross overlooking Aherlow and offers perhaps the most stunning view in the south of Ireland. Not only is it possible to see the County Waterford coast and several nearby mountain ranges but also, on a day of perfect visibility, the view extends from the Wicklow Mountains in the east to the unmistakably slender outline of Carrauntoohil, in County Kerry.

To descend, first traverse Galtymore's west summit, then walk southwest across a plateau known as Dawson's Table. Next follow an expansive spur that descends roughly southeast without undue steepness to the confluence of two streams. Cross both and follow a well-defined track that initially skirts a wood but then strikes uphill across moorland to rejoin the Black Road about 400m beyond the previously encountered second gate. Now retrace your steps downhill to your parking place.

Overleaf: *Looking from Knocknafillia summit plateau towards Knocknagnauv with Knockmealdown and Knockmoylan in the background*

THE KNOCKMEALDOWN MOUNTAINS

When Robert Lloyd Praeger encountered the Knockmealdown Mountains on his famous exploration of the Irish landscape, he was not overly impressed. 'There is nothing except this single row of summits – no lakes or corries, deep glens or cliffs; very little bare rock:' Quite apart from the fact that he was obviously incorrect – Bay Lough is a fine example of a corrie lake at the heart of the Knockmealdowns – he was probably also just a bit unfair.

Sure, the Knockmealdowns have been rather too generously planted with conifers, are overshadowed by the higher Galtees and lack the rugged grandeur of the Comeragh coums, but they should, nevertheless, not be ignored by the discerning hillwalker for in every respect they form a proper mountain range. These tranquil highlands are also very accessible as they are bisected by three scenic roads through high mountain passes and also by the Glengalla stream valley, which divides the central Knockmealdowns but can only be traversed on foot.

A visit to the Knockmealdowns rewards the walker with well-defined peaks offering excellent viewpoints, some of the least-wet underfoot conditions in Ireland and an inescapable feeling of getting away from it all on less frequented summits that seem to encapsulate the true freedom of the hills.

WALK 15
BAY LOUGH AND SUGARLOAF MOUNTAIN

START:
Walk begins from the parking place beside the first hairpin bend beyond Clogheen on the R668.

Time:
Allow 4½ hours for the longer route, 3 hours for the shorter route.

Map:
OSi Sheet 74.

Suitability:
A moderate challenge for walkers with a reasonable level of fitness. In mist it may be better for those without navigational skills to return to the R668 by the route of ascent, using the earthen bank as a guide.

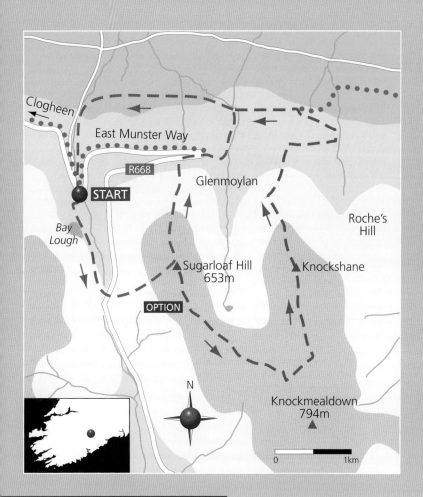

Cloghaan

East Munster Way

R668

START

Bay Lough

Glenmoylan

Roche's Hill

Sugarloaf Hill 653m

Knockshane

OPTION

N

Knockmealdown 794m

0   1km

Bay Lough and Sugarloaf Mountain

For generations of children from the south midlands, mention of the word 'Vee' created an inevitable quickening of the pulse. In less affluent times, when young people were still allowed to make playgrounds of the fields and woodlands of rural Ireland, crossing the Vee counted as a high adventure to the exotic coastal lands beyond the Knockmealdown Mountains. There lay the great Cistercian abbey of Mount Melleray and the promise of exploring its famous groves and enjoying 'meat tea' and currant cake from kindly but resolutely unspeaking monks. In summer the journey usually concluded at the ultimate childhood nirvana – Clonea Beach, outside Dungarvan.

The switchback road across the Vee, which made such family adventures possible, was constructed for Famine Relief in the 1840s. Today it offers one of

The Grubb Monument on the flank of Sugarloaf Mountain

Ireland's outstanding scenic drives as it meanders between the Sugarloaf Mountain standing sentinel above Bay Lough's lonesome curl of water. Hiking opportunities abound in an area that is renowned for its rich folklore and abundant historic resonances.

From your starting point **S027 113** (see panel above) follow a stony track uphill through dense vegetation. In June the area is a riot of pink-flowering rhododendrons. Visitors observing the luxuriant spectacle are mostly unaware that this seemingly attractive shrub is actually a considerable woodland pest. It forms impenetrable thickets that now threaten the fragile ecosystems of many forest areas.

In about 15 minutes you reach the point where glaciation has re-engineered the mountain to create brooding Bay Lough. It is unlikely that you will see bathers here though, for a deeply held local tradition warns that the ghostly arm of the

Footbridge over the Glenmoylan stream, which is crossed on the alternative route ('Option') below

witch, Petticoat Loose, will rise from her resting place in the depths to ensnare those bold enough to enter these lonesome waters. Such tales do, of course, tend to bend historic facts to suit the requirements of the age. In reality, Petticoat Loose was a local woman named Mary Hannigan whose crime was, in all probability, not witchcraft, but that of daring to be different in misogynistic times.

Go left along the lakeshore and continue upwards on a broad track following a pre-Famine road. Here you should try to step back in time and let your imagination soar until the nineteenth-century long cars and sweating horses of the Italian emigrant Charles Bianconi are once again toiling upwards on rutted roads to the head of the Gap. Bianconi was in many ways the Michael O'Leary of his day and created Ireland's first low-cost system of transportation for ordinary people. At the end of the track a strange stone building beside the road is where his horses rested after the demanding haul upwards from Clogheen.

Now cross the road and follow an earthen bank marking the boundary between counties Tipperary and Waterford, which leads steeply uphill on the west flank of Sugarloaf Mountain. It is strenuous going now for about 45 minutes until you ascend a final rise to encounter a rough drystone wall and head left for the south and highest summit of Sugarloaf (663m) with its incongruously English name marking it out from nearly all the other Knockmealdown peaks that clearly have names rooted in Gaelic.

If you have developed a serious walking habit, however, and would prefer a longer outing, this is the place you diverge – see alternative route below. Whichever route you choose, however, your effort is presently well rewarded, for the Sugarloaf is embellished by twin stony summits that offer exquisite views across Tipperary's Golden Vale to the distant bulk of the Galtee Mountains.

Having imbibed fully of the vista, descend north from the northern summit by way of a rather indistinct track. You should now be heading towards the R668 at a point just left of a hairpin bend. Continue descending until a curious structure is encountered just above the road. This beehive-like edifice marks the last resting place of William Grubb, a landowner from a distinguished Quaker family with extensive holdings in nearby Castlegrace who died in 1922. Tradition holds that the curious shape of his mausoleum was determined by the fact that Grubb insisted on being buried in an upright position, to keep a better eye on his property interests.

From here descend to the road and follow the R668 about 200m (right) to a hairpin bend. Leave the road at this bend and follow the directional arrows from a signpost marked 'spur to the East Munster Way' along a stony track. After a short distance the track divides and you take the left (downhill) option. The track now meanders downwards to join the Tipperary Heritage Way and the East Munster Way near an attractive wooden footbridge. Do not cross this bridge but instead follow the signs for the Tipperary Heritage Way (as described in the alternative route below) all the way back to your start point.

Option

Once you encounter the drystone wall after your ascent from the Vee Gap do not go left along the Sugarloaf's summit but instead swing right. From here there are few navigational difficulties as you continue along the broad crest beside the wall as it alternates with an earthen ditch while continuing to mark the border between counties Tipperary and Waterford. It provides a perfect navigation handrail as it ascends like a giant staircase for less than an hour until you reach the high col immediately below the summit of Knockmealdown Mountain. Here, instead of ascending Knockmealdown you swing northeast towards Knockmoylan, which is shown as point 768m on the OSi map and is marked by a pile of stones. Next head down the broad, heathery Knockshane spur past another cairn. Then aim to keep a little left of the spur as the descent steepens and afterwards you encounter a well-constructed path skirting a forest edge.

Follow this path right until it dives into the trees and continue descending past the corner of a clear-felled area to reach a broad turning circle. From here take a wide forest roadway as it first heads east then roughly north and finally west. At a Y-junction take the right-hand path (lower option) and very soon you will encounter signs for the Tipperary Heritage Way, which at this point has coalesced with the East Munster Way.

Follow the waymarkers to the left and continue until they reach a three-way junction. Go left here until the forest roadway loops left again, which is your cue to take a right and cross a pretty footbridge over the Glenmoylan stream. The terrain changes sharply here as you encounter open scrubland before entering another forest. Continue following the arrows along a wide forest service road until, at the end of a long straight stretch, the trail swings left. Immediately afterwards you part company with the East Munster Way, which heads right while you continue by following the waymarkers for the Tipperary Heritage Way until the forest roadway goes left. Here you continue ahead on a much narrower green trail through luxuriant rhododendron shrubs. If the time happens to be late May or early June, the entire area will be an exuberant blaze of exhilarating purple. Eventually you emerge from the forest onto the R668 with the picturesque bridge beside your parking place immediately to the right.

Rhododendron in full bloom near the Tipperary Heritage Way

WALK 16
THE CENTRAL KNOCKMEALDOWNS

START:
The village of Goatenbridge – shown inexplicably as 'Goat's Br' on the OSi map – is located about 3 miles west of Newcastle village. From this tiny hamlet, containing just a shop and a large pub, follow a minor road south to a three-way junction, where there is an intersection with the East Munster Way. There is plenty of parking space here and this is the start point for your walk.

Time:
6 hours.

Map:
OSi Sheet 74.

Suitability:
A demanding walk requiring good levels of fitness. Good route-finding skills are also required where the route departs from the navigational handrail of the Knockmealdown embankment.

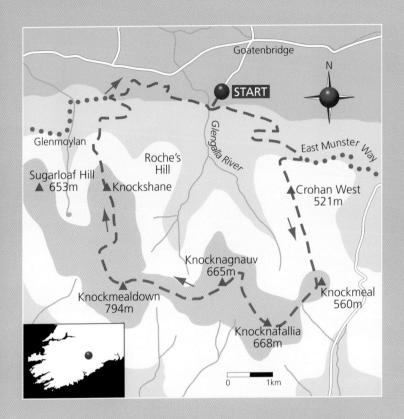

The Central Knockmealdowns

If there is a mountain circuit in Ireland that could justifiably be described as knocking on heaven's door, the full circuit of the central Knockmealdowns must surely claim the distinction. The reason is not that this fine route straddling the border between Tipperary and Waterford possesses some of Ireland's most elevated uplands or highest peaks, for it does not. Instead, virtually every summit here comes with the initial moniker 'knock' attached.

Begin your walk at **S080 121** (see panel above) and follow the signs (left) for the East Munster Way and the Liam Lynch Monument. If any of the signs happen to be missing the sequence to follow is: right option at the first junction, left at the next and then left again before continuing straight ahead to reach the entrance to the Liam Lynch Monument. This is a 20m-high memorial in the form of a round tower erected in 1935 to the memory of Liam Lynch, the chief of staff of the anti-treaty forces during the Irish Civil War. The sad events that took place here neatly encapsulate the huge tragedy that was the Irish Civil War. The

View from Knocknafillia towards Knockmeal   *The Liam Lynch Monument*

monument marks the location where Lynch was wounded in a gun battle and then captured on 10 April 1923 by former comrades who were now members of the Free State Army.

Despite the fact that he was a bitter and deadly opponent of those who accepted the treaty with Britain, the soldiers made every effort to save the badly wounded Lynch. Laboriously they carried their former comrade using an improvised stretcher on the long journey down the mountainside to Nugent's Pub in Newcastle village. From here he was transferred by ambulance to Clonmel Hospital where he succumbed to his wounds. Before passing away, however, he presented his captors with a gold pen as a poignant symbol of respect for the erstwhile companions he had served with in the War of Independence. And Ireland's strong consciousness of its history has ensured that Lynch has not been forgotten. Almost eight decades after his death, a large crowd still congregates here each year, on a July Sunday, for a Liam Lynch commemoration.

From the Lynch Monument follow a difficult-to-detect trail that runs roughly west from the monument and enters the forest. At the edge of the trees go left along a narrow track that leads to open mountainside. Now it is just a question of taking the track upwards as it follows a line of disused fence posts to reach the summit of Crohan West (521m). Since this summit is an outlier at the northern extremity of the Knockmealdowns there are sublime views to the Comeraghs, Slievenamon and the Galtee Mountains.

Two low walls extend from Crohan West. Take the one on the left and follow it through often tedious underfoot conditions. The wall, and sometimes embankment, run more or less in a straight line on the west side of the ridge crest to Knockmeal (560m) where it is necessary to divert left more than 100m to visit the summit cairn.

Now rejoin the embankment, which denotes the boundary between Tipperary and Waterford, and descend easily to a col that marks the upper end of the Glengalla River valley. Here you have a choice to follow the embankment as it rises and then dog-legs to reach the summit of Knocknagnauv. But this is to ignore Knocknafallia, which is one of the best viewpoints on the route. So leave the security of the embankment and pursue a faint track straight ahead and sharply upwards to reach the summit plateau (668m). This is embellished by a widely separated prehistoric burial mound and a stone cairn.

Head to the burial mound – which has been disturbed to create a shelter – and enjoy outrageously photogenic views over the great meandering River Blackwater to the silvery outline of the southern ocean beyond. Directly below is the rather dreamy outline of the renowned Cistercian abbey of Mount Melleray. The original Melleray Abbey was located in Brittany until its monks were expelled from France in 1830. Taking advantage of religious emancipation, which took place in 1829, they came to Ireland under the leadership of Abbot Vincent Ryan. They briefly settled at Rathmore, County Kerry, before founding a new Mount Melleray among the foothills of the Knockmealdown Mountains.

Now traverse the flat summit plateau to the stone cairn and then descend to the col between Knocknafallia and Knocknagnauv to pick up the embankment once again and follow it until it becomes a stone wall near Knocknagnauv summit (665m). Your roller-coaster ride continues now as you descend to the next broad col that is bisected by the ancient Rinn Bó Phadraig ('furrow of Patrick's cow'). Legend has it that the route was created by a cow owned by St Patrick charging up the mountain in pursuit of a stolen calf. In fact, it is most likely an ancient trail linking royal Cashel with the major ecclesiastical centre at Ardmore.

Now follow the stiffest ascent of the day where you rise 240m to the summit of Knockmealdown Mountain (794m), the highest point in the eponymous range. The mountaintop is marked by a trig point and offers extensive views in all directions. Next descend northwest to a col where you part company with the comforting presence of the embankment/wall for the final time.

Instead you swing northeast and track the route as described in Walk 15 ('Option') over Knockmoylan and down the Knockshane spur to reach eventually the East Munster and Tipperary Heritage Ways. Here, instead of following the signs left, swing right to trail the walking arrows eastwards along a well-surfaced forest roadway.

When you arrive at a large turning circle, the route scuttles left into the forest. You now pursue a much narrower trail passing over a stream by way of a simple log-pole bridge to emerge finally from the wood at a solid forest road where you turn right. Then just follow the walking arrows by taking the left option at each junction to eventually cross a well-constructed bridge over the Glengalla River and soon after reach the start point of your walk.

WALK 17
KNOCKSHANAHULLION AND THE WESTERN KNOCKMEALDOWNS

START:
Walk begins from the parking place below the statue of Our Lady of Knock at the highest point of the Vee Gap between Clogheen and Lismore on the R668.

Time:
4½ hours for the full route. For the shorter route, allow 2½ hours.

Map:
OSi Sheet 74.

Suitability:
A moderate challenge for walkers with a reasonable level of fitness. The helpful arrows of the Blackwater Way and an extensive network of well-maintained fences aid but do not eliminate the need for navigation skills.

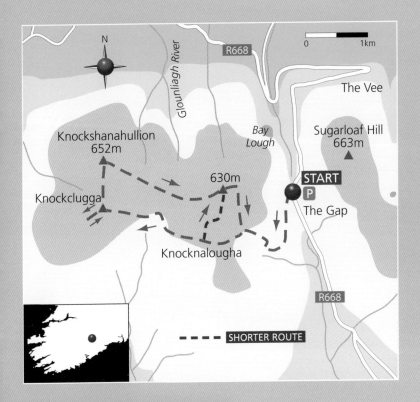

Map labels: N, Glounliagh River, R668, The Vee, Knockshanahullion 652m, Bay Lough, Sugarloaf Hill 663m, 630m, START P, The Gap, Knockclugga, Knocknalougha, R668, 0 — 1km, SHORTER ROUTE

Knockshanahullion and the Western Knockmealdowns

Are some of your best memories from carefree days when, in the style of Wordsworth, you 'wandered lonely as a cloud' through swathes of beguiling countryside? Certainly this was true of famous English Lakeland walker and guidebook writer Alfred W. Wainwright. AW so loved the solitude of the hills that he spoke on the BBC *Desert Island Discs* programme of dodging behind a rock when he encountered other walkers.

If you believe Wordsworth and Wainwright had it right and that the uplands are best sampled in solitude it may be that your ship has now sailed. Hillwalking has never been more popular in Ireland and you are now unlikely to find true solitude on any of Ireland's most popular trails. Fortunately, however, there are still places in Ireland where you can ramble through a refreshingly less-frequented landscape where most likely you won't meet another soul. The gentle western hills of the Knockmealdown Mountains are presently one such example.

To explore the landscape to the west of lonesome Bay Lough leave the car park at the highest point of the Vee Gap at **S030 101** and go directly towards a shrine to Our Lady of Knock. Continue contouring southwest past the statue

Looking towards Knockmealdown Mountain from point 630m in the west Knockmealdowns

to join a more distinct track rising uphill. You now follow the waymarkers for the Avondhu section of the Blackwater Way on a pleasant trail with forestry to the left until the track begins descending, which is your cue to go immediately right to join a track heading west.

Follow this switchback track to a point where three fences intersect. Here, for some reason, the waymarkers point away from the forest edge to follow a soft peaty mountain path that hugs a fence as it rises on the flanks of Knocknalougha and then descends to join a well-constructed roadway skirting a forest. If you prefer a shorter outing or are not confident of your navigation skills and prefer the security of a 'handrail', track the waymarkers from here until a fence leads right. Follow this, going first right and then left at the fence intersections to reach the splendid views from point 630m. From here, return as set out later in this route description.

On my rambles I usually take the longer route by diverging here from the Blackwater Way. To reduce mountain erosion and enjoy more amenable underfoot conditions I instead continue from the three-fence intersection along the existing trail that skirts the forest. I then take the first right and later the right option at the next three-way junction to rejoin the waymarkers for the Blackwater Way.

Whichever way you choose, you end up on a firm wide pathway with a forest to the left. Now it is a question of keeping on the trail by the forest edge

Looking south over the Vee Gap from Knockalougha

until a large white stile crosses a fence ahead leading to open moorland. Marker poles now denote the way as the route climbs steeply to reach the summit of Knockclugga, which is hardly a distinct mountaintop but more a spur to the south of Knockshanahullion. When you reach its highest point say goodbye to the Blackwater Way and head north along a broad ridge with gently rising ground to reach Knockshanahullion (652m) the highest point in the west Comeraghs. The summit is crowned by a trig pillar and a large burial cairn which has been disrupted to create a stone shelter. There are also some standing stone arrangements that are clearly of modern construction.

When you have imbibed sufficiently of the excellent views especially north to the Galtee Mountains and south to the Waterford coast, descend steeply at first in a southeasterly direction heading towards the corner of a fence. Follow this fence east but when it swings south, strike out east towards point 630m. Do not follow a direct route, however, but arc a little to the south to avoid losing height in the steep valley of the upper Glounliagh River. As you near the summit you should pick up a faint mountain track. The summit is crowned by a cairn and there are impressive views east to the Sugarloaf and Knockmealdown Ridge.

Now continue east for a couple of hundred metres following a fence. When another fence leads south follow this and continue all the way with a gradual descent to reach the intersection of three fences encountered earlier. Now just retrace your steps back to your starting point.

Looking from Tountinna over Laghtea Hill to Lough Derg

THE ARRA MOUNTAINS

Mountains have always been special places. Down through the ages, succeeding generations have ascribed legend to them and credited them with powers of spirituality and magic. It is the enigmatic quality of high places, their prominence and permanence against our transience and triviality that draws us to them.

Nowhere is this truer than among the compact huddle of hills that lies west of Nenagh. Here people have lived and farmed close to the summits for countless generations with the result that evidence of human endeavour is everywhere. And the gentle Arra Mountains are still people-friendly, with benign slopes and the many criss-crossing trails footed by previous generations now bidding present-day walkers come hither. A dense concentration of historic artefacts, mythological resonances and evidence of previous commercial exploitation then awaits to be uncovered by those who merely take the time to stop and stare.

WALK 18
THE MILLENNIUM CROSS AND TOUNTINNA

START:
From Nenagh follow the R494 through the village of Portroe to reach, on the right-hand side, the prominent viewing point and car park known as at 'The Lookout' where there is ample parking. The walk begins from here.

Time:
4 hours.

Map:
OSi Sheet 59.

Suitability:
The route has one steepish section but generally it presents few objective dangers or navigational difficulties. Nevertheless, walkers should have good footwear and carry warm clothing.

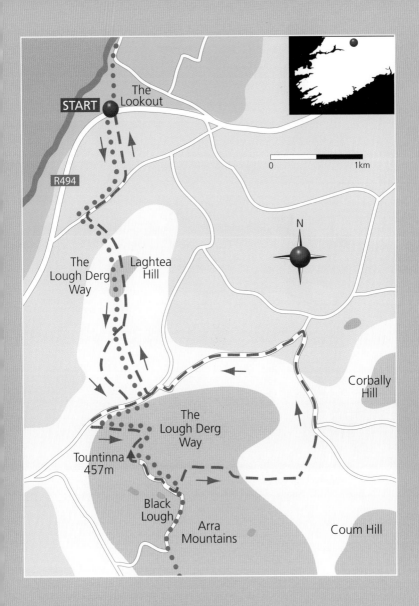

START

The Lookout

R494

The Lough Derg Way

Laghtea Hill

N

0   1km

Corbally Hill

The Lough Derg Way

Tountinna 457m

Black Lough

Arra Mountains

Coum Hill

The Millennium Cross and Tountinna

Walkers approaching the Millennium Cross on the summit of Laghtea Hill while taking part in the Nenagh Walking Festival

For a real feeling of regressing in time begin your Arra Mountains walk from a viewing point known locally as 'The Lookout' at **R734 810**. This is located on the road between Ballina and Portroe and offers an opportunity to savour memorable views over island-littered Lough Derg. From here, follow the waymarkers for the Lough Derg Way (note that the route has been altered since the OSi map was published) through bucolic fields and lanes to reach a road where the arrows point you to the right for about 600m. Then it is left and upwards on a pleasant rustic lane. You meander through a disused slate quarry, which acts as a reminder that until relatively recently these hills were a commercial hub. Before the sun set on the natural slate industry in the last century, slate-quarrying employed up to 500 people in the Arras with 15,000 tons of slate transported annually through Killaloe.

It is upwards now as you cross a metal bridge and follow a fence and later a low ditch to reach the summit of Laghtea Hill. Locally known as Cloneybrien, the summit bears the remains of a cross that was erected here in the 1930s and subsequently destroyed by lightning. A large metal Millennium Cross replaced it in 2005.

Descend now by continuing to follow the Lough Derg Way for just over 1km to reach a tarmacadam roadway and go right for about 500m until the waymarkers point left and uphill.

Where the path leaves the road a conclave of large stones forms a historical site that is commonly referred to as 'the Graves of the Leinstermen'. This moniker reputedly dates from Brian Boru's kingship of Munster when the hero of Clontarf supposedly showed himself as the ultimate tenth-century father-in-law from hell. His soldiers, according to legend, ambushed and massacred the King of Leinster and his entourage at this site as he travelled to request the hand of Brian's daughter in marriage. Myths, of course, tend to rearrange facts to mesh with later beliefs and in reality this site is of Bronze Age origin and, therefore, pre-dates Brian Boru by about 2,000 years.

Next comes sustained upward mobility along a rising zigzag path on Tountinna ('hill of the wave') – supposedly named after a biblical flood that, according to the ancient Book of Invasions, drowned all of the first Irish inhabitants.

The well-signposted but less-than-well-maintained Graves of the Leinstermen

However, there was one survivor named Fionntán, who cannily took refuge high on Tountinna and thereby lived to recount the tale.

The summit experience on Tountinna (457m) is initially lessened by huge, ugly, micro-link repeater, or deflector, masts that dominate the skyline. Whenever I approach a summit such as Tountinna, I can't help reflecting on the fate of these masts when advancing satellite technology eventually renders them obsolete. Will they then be dismantled and the mountaintop returned to its former pristine state? Or will they be regarded as having become sufficiently integrated into the landscape to earn a preservation order as eye-grabbing monuments to cruder past technologies? I hope it's the former, but whatever the answer it is for the present necessary to look past these intrusive artefacts to savour the summit vista. You will then be well compensated, for this mountaintop is a photographer's dream with magical views to the Clare hills across the aquamarine waters of serene Lough Derg.

From the summit continue following the Lough Derg Way until a small lake (Black Lough) appears to the right. Abandon the waymarkers here and go left towards yet another communications tower and then left again to follow a broad path skirting a forest. After a few hundred metres, cross a ditch on the right to enter woodland. This turning is easily missed so the grid reference here is **R74100 75564**. Now follow a pleasant sylvan trail leading mostly downhill. At a three-way junction go left and continue along a broad forest roadway to reach yet another junction where again the left option is taken. Continue descending along the forest roadway with disused slate quarries and an artificial lake now industrialising the horizon ahead until an asphalt road is reached. Turn left and continue for a few hundred metres to reach a T–Junction. Again go left and somewhat uphill past several spoil heaps from the slate industry to reach the entrance to the still-operational Killoran Slate Quarries.

At this point the tarmacadam gives way to an unpaved rustic path leading to another junction. Take the left option here and soon after go right where a sign says 'Millennium Cross 1,200m'. Now it is simply a question of retracing your steps over Laghtea Hill and then following the Lough Derg Way back to your start point at The Lookout.

OTHER WALKS

WALK 19
SLIEVENAMON

START:

Heading from Clonmel to Kilkenny on the N76, branch left for Ballypatrick after about 12km. Turn right and go through Kilcash, following signs for Slievenamon summit, until the entrance to a stony lane is reached where there is plenty of roadside parking.

Time:

The up-and-down route can be done in 2 hours. For the extended circuit, allow an additional 2 hours.

Map:

OSi Sheets 67 and 75.

Suitability:

Ascent/descent by Kilcash track is suitable if you are of only moderate fitness. On the extended circuit, the terrain crosses featureless upland with sometimes disagreeable heather so you need to be averagely fit. Navigation skills are also required on a misty day.

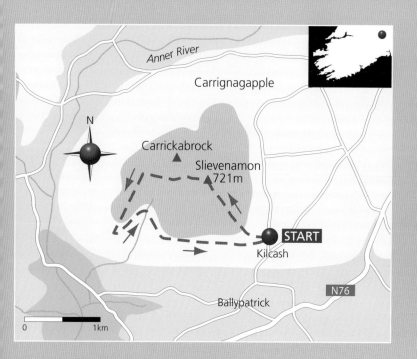

People above a certain age will immediately recognise the melody. Once this ballad routinely reverberated around Croke Park on the first Sunday of September, compliments of the Artane Boys' Band. Those were the days when Doyle-, Maher- and Stakelum-powered Tipperary teams claimed All-Ireland hurling success with monotonous regularity.

Since then things have moved on. In the age of equality we now have the more politically correct Artane Band and Premier County stickmen have found it exasperatingly difficult to reclaim former glories. Slievenamon, however, remains as a constant, still laying undisputed claim to the title of quintessential Tipperary mountain, with the familiar lyrics 'Alone, all alone' guaranteed a syrupy rendition wherever Tipp folk mingle around the globe.

Alone in song and alone by location, Slievemamon is the place where County Tipperary secretes its soul and is an ever-present and unmistakable backdrop to the landscape at the southern end of the county. With sensuously feminine shoulders that curve gently to a much-visited summit, this solitary peak provides much to justify its ancient title as the 'Mountain of Women'.

To ascend Slievenamon, follow a stony lane located above Kilcash (see panel above) which starts at **S317 288**. You will soon pass through two gates to open mountainside. Swing immediately right here past a simple cross, erected

Walkers descending the summit track of Slievenamon

to commemorate a pilgrimage to the mountain's summit that took place to mark the year 2000.

Now an obvious stony track, which initially runs parallel to a forest, climbs over a low rise and then heads directly for the summit. The going is never difficult but is somewhat demanding on the lungs. Halfway up you will probably be glad to turn around to catch your breath and gaze upon the vista of the castellated Suir Valley lying below with the Comeragh Mountains beyond. Directly beneath, your eyes will be drawn to the ruins of Kilcash Castle, once a great stronghold of the Butlers. An unknown muse recorded the fall of this great house around 1650 with a poem that features the well-known opening lines *'Cad a dhéanfaimid feasta gan adhmad?'* It is still studied by schoolchildren as a poignant lament for the decline of Gaelic Ireland, and you might while away the time on the last leg of your ascent by trying to recall the remaining words.

Surprisingly for such a salient peak there is no cross crowning the summit (721m) but as compensation there is huge burial cairn, reputed to contain the entrance to the Celtic underworld. A depression in the rocks is believed to be Fionn MacCumhail's seat, from which he watched candidates for his hand in marriage race to the summit. Legend has it that he cheated and helped his favourite, Gráinne, to win. Apparently she was unimpressed by such chivalry. During the subsequent wedding banquet she eloped with Diarmuid, thereby creating the material for the tragic melodrama of Diarmuid and Gráinne.

Slievenamon has a flattened top, and so to appreciate the full view it is necessary to circle the summit plateau. Do this on a clear day and the tableaux of east Munster and south Leinster appear beneath. On all sides fertile plains haze away to distant ranges. North and east are the Blackstairs, the Slieve Blooms and Slievefelim Hills. West and south are the Galtee, Knockmealdown and Comeragh Mountains to complete the upland necklace.

At this stage you may return by the route of your ascent. If you are inclined to exercise further, strike out across the heathery mountainside in a westerly direction. At first you descend quite rapidly, then the moorland terrain levels out and soon rises gently again.

After about 2.5km Killusty Cross, erected to commemorate the 1950 Holy Year, will appear ahead. If you decide not to make the there-and-back detour to the cross, bear left, following the crest of a sometimes bouldery ridge until a steepish descent brings you to a track at right angles to your descent, which skirts a forest.

Follow this left and downhill to cross a stream and then continue upwards on an undulating stony path that continues skirting the forest on your right. The track traverses a small ravine and then continues to a point where the forest edge swings sharply right. Abandon the forest at this stage and strike directly ahead on a track that traverses open mountainside with forest now well below you. Continue over a stream to reach the corner of a drystone wall and a junction with another track coming from the right. From here it is plain sailing along an agreeable trail to the commemorative cross encountered earlier and then down the stony lane to your parking place.

Kilcash Castle

WALK 20
THE SLIEVENAMUCK CIRCUIT

START:
From Tipperary town take the R664 for Aherlow. Soon after negotiating a couple of hairpin bends the entrance to Aherlow House Hotel is signposted to the right.

Time:
2½ hours.

Map:
OSi Sheet 66.

Suitability:
The walk offers little in terms of objective dangers and has been successfully completed by children as young as six.

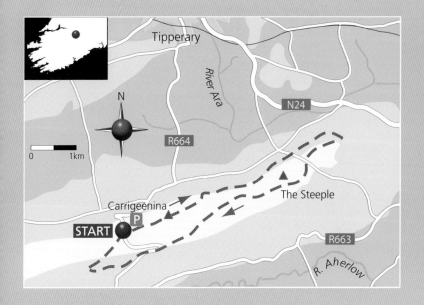

The hidden Ireland of John Hinde postcards, so popular with generations of tourists, has been reduced by Ireland's now departed years of affluence to a mouldy metaphor for a supposedly simpler, happier Ireland. And in many ways this is a good thing, for only green-tinged American visitors and urbanised locals – safely removed from the back-breaking reality of subsistence farming – still long for the nostalgic landscapes of a mythical Ireland. The supposedly idyllic lifestyle of thatched homes, ass-and-cart agriculture, road-roaming sheep flocks and farm families eking a precarious living from the land was terminated long ago by the EU, the JCB and the microprocessor.

These days the Irish countryside is a place of pristine modern houses, productive farms and hugely expanded villages. And amid such rapid change there are, of course, many egregious examples where we have been irresponsible with concrete blocks, created ugly ribbon developments and irreversibly reduced the quality of the environment. Search carefully, however, and you will find places removed from urban hubs and tourism honey pots where life still moves at a slower, gentler pace, buildings relax easily into the backdrop and the lure of the landscape remains undiminished.

West Tipperary has such a place – a secluded glen that has resolutely defended its charm against the worst excesses of our once rampant Celtic Tiger. And above the Glen of Aherlow, the sylvan Slievenamuck Ridge offers an easy but memorable walk that is well suited for families and proffers breathtaking views to the Galtee Mountains.

The walk starts in the car park beside Aherlow House Hotel **R870 304** (see panel above), which was originally built as a hunting lodge and has retained its old world charm. From here follow the tarred road east and uphill to the entrance for the hotel. Next cross the road to the car park opposite and follow the track, signposted 'Rock an Thorabh' ('rock of the bull') for about 1.5km. The Rock lies about 40m left of the trail and is a wonderful viewing point for the Golden Vale, Tipperary town and the Slievefelim Hills beyond.

Continue along the Slievenamuck Ridge, which is named after a fearsome sow that is reputed to have been put to the spear by no less an individual than Fionn McCumhaill. When you reach a point where four tracks intersect take the left option and continue downhill for 1km until a minor public road is crossed. Continue on the path directly opposite for another 1km to a junction where the track swings very sharply right and almost backwards.

This leads to a tarmac road, which you follow to the left for 100m to the unmistakable Jubilee 2000 Memorial that was constructed as a joint project between the parishes of Tipperary and Bansha Kilmoyler to celebrate the Millennium Year. Designed by sculptor Jarlath Daly, the stone depicts the Annunciation, Birth, Crucifixion and Resurrection from the life of Christ and makes an excellent place for a food break.

Once replenished, head off by following the track directly opposite the memorial. As you ascend you will enjoy splendid views across the Glen of Aherlow to the mighty Galtee Mountains. At the next junction continue straight ahead on a narrow and sometimes mucky track that ascends and then descends steeply to the four-way junction encountered earlier. This time you take the left option. After approximately 2km you will come to a parking place and viewing point, which is overlooked by a large statue of Christ the King, right hand raised in magisterial blessing to the glen below.

Follow the main road directly ahead for about 100m to the other end of the viewing area where a path leads down wooden steps into the Glen of Aherlow Nature Reserve. This is an admirable local community initiative and consists of over 40 acres of diverse, natural woodland with a well-illustrated nature trail. Follow the arrows through the reserve until a wooden stile leads onto a broad lane as it descends to an attractive stone bridge. You are now standing on an old coach road, which was used by the long cars of Italian immigrant Charles Bianconi who set up Ireland's first system of mass transportation.

From this bridge descend to another intersection where you go right and then simply foot it the short distance back to your parking place. Here you might say thank-you for the parking facilities by popping into Aherlow House and enjoying a cuppa and a bite in the suitably elegant surroundings of the Hunting Lodge Bar.

Walkers enjoying a ramble on the woodland paths of Slievenamuck

WALK 21
THE CRAG LOOP

START:
Mazes of small roads straddle the Tipperary/Kilkenny border and this means that the tiny village of Grange is not the easiest to find. To locate the trailhead, head for Urlingford and take the R690, signposted Mullinahone. After 2km stay on the R690 as the road divides and continue for almost 5km, passing the entrance to Kilcooley Estate. Beyond Kilcooley take the first left, following the estate wall, and after 2km you will enter Grange village. The trailhead is located outside Hogan's Pub.

Time:
2 hours.

Map:
OSi Sheet 67 (however, it is not really necessary).

Suitability:
This is a pleasant and unchallenging walk along dry woodland trails that is readily accomplished wearing trainers. It makes for an ideal family outing.

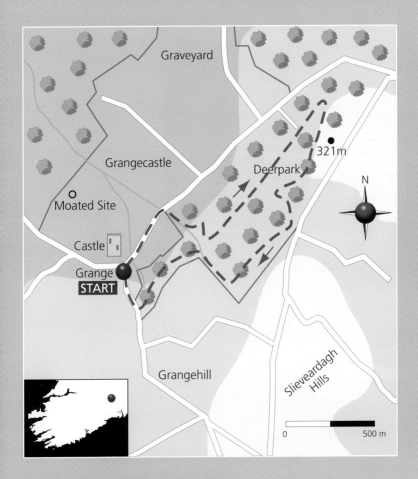

The Crag Loop

Perhaps you have spent a little too much time in the fast-food lane, but now your priorities are all about pulse-raising self-improvement and rewarding excursions to the outdoors. But while you would appreciate a little more familiarity with the Irish uplands, rambling is your game and you're happy to leave the intensity of near vertical landscapes to dedicated mountain lovers.

Don't worry, however, for there is now a loop walk at the beating heart of rural Tipperary that simply aches for footfall. The newly developed Crag Loop makes an ideal introduction to green exercising and is an outing calculated to entice even the most committed of couch potatoes into the great outdoors.

Lying close to the Kilkenny border, it explores a most amenable landscape as it saunters through some of the original woodlands of the Kilcooley Abbey estate and makes an ideal antidote for those suffering 'nature deficit disorder'.

The Wellington Monument

This estate, nestling within a green and fertile landscape on the edge of the Slieveardagh Hills, was home to the Ponsonby/Barker family from the 1770s until recently and still holds many compelling resonances from the ascendancy period of Irish history.

To complete this straightforward circuit, start from outside Hogan's Pub at **S307 564** in the tiny village of Grange. Follow the purple arrows along the metalled road for 500m to reach the entrance to Grangecrag Woods (right). Take this woodland track to reach an incongruous-looking building on the right that once served as the deep freeze for the Kilcooley estate. Blocks of ice were cut from frozen ponds or rivers nearby and transported to what was then known as the icehouse, where they were stacked between layers of straw to create a microclimate. Ice, so preserved, could keep throughout the summer and this particular icehouse was used as a cold store for Kilcooley from the eighteenth to mid-twentieth centuries.

Continue from the icehouse to reach a three-way junction where the arrows are followed right. Ascend along the forest road to reach another three-way junction where you turn a sharp left onto a forestry road that ascends for about a 1km to reach a T-junction where you again go right.

Walk on for about another 5 minutes until a track on the left takes you uphill to reach a large odd-to-behold construction known locally as the Wellington Monument. It was built in 1817 by William Barker of the Kilcooley Estate to commemorate the victory of the Duke of Wellington at the Battle of Waterloo in 1815. Such buildings are generally referred to as follies but usually they served a purpose. Here the idea was clearly to provide a focus to draw people to the highest point of the estate where they would then be impressed by fine views of the great house and sylvan glories of the parkland laid out below. Today these views are hidden by a stand of timber, but the local community now has plans to overcome this obstacle by creating a viewing point at the top of the monument under a recently inaugurated 'adopt a monument' scheme.

Now continue following the arrows along the forest road to a junction with another metalled road where you veer immediately right to re-enter a forest trail. After about 500m the route veers left and crosses open ground where you now enjoy the previously obscured views to the great house at Kilcooley and the extensive ruins of the nearby twelfth-century Cistercian abbey. Beyond these, the Devilsbit Mountain provides a compelling backdrop to this serene, pastoral panorama.

Soon after, you enter mature broadleaf woodland and swing right to descend by a stream to exit onto a track. Continue (left) following green and purple arrows along the woodland track for almost 1km to reach a tarred roadway. Turn right and downhill here and soon after you are back at the trailhead in Grange.

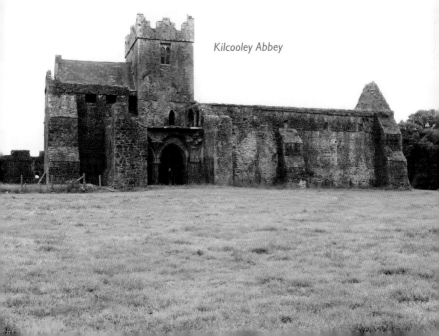

Kilcooley Abbey

WALK 22
DEVILSBIT MOUNTAIN

START:
Leave Templemore along the R501 towards Borrisoleigh and at a crossroads follow the signs right for Barnane. Continue following the signs marked Borrisnafarney that point straight ahead at the next crossroads. When the road reaches its highest point, there is parking at a large gateway on the right.

Time:
Allow under 2 hours for the shorter walk, 3 hours for the extended walk.

Map:
OSi Sheet 59.

Suitability:
A generally unchallenging outing suitable for those with moderate fitness. The mountaintop is, however, quite exposed so be prepared with spare clothing and raingear. Great care should also be taken ascending and descending the steep cliffs surrounding the Little Rock and also descending from the Long Rock plateau.

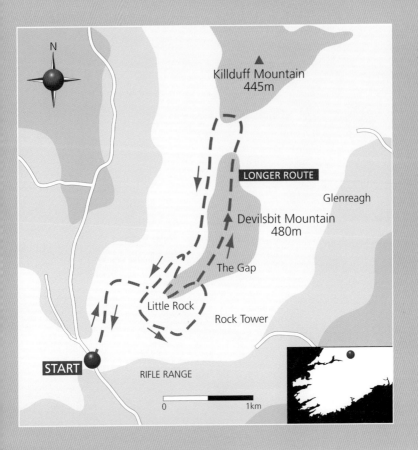

N

▲ Killduff Mountain
445m

LONGER ROUTE

Glenreagh

▲ Devilsbit Mountain
480m

The Gap

Little Rock

Rock Tower

START

RIFLE RANGE

0   1km

Devilsbit Mountain

In many ways it is one of our best-known mountains. Generations of travellers on the Dublin–Cork railway line have gazed in fascination at the unmistakeable gash in its flat summit that is clearly visible above Templemore. Other salient Irish peaks that inescapably draw the eye in the same way, such as Brandon, Croagh Patrick and Slieve Gullion, have attracted a mixture of superstition and worship for countless centuries. In this regard Tipperary's Devilsbit Mountain is no exception.

A charming legend holds that a fleeing demon, being pursued out of Ireland by St Patrick, took an angry bite from its summit plateau and later dropped it to form the Rock of Cashel. Unfortunately, scientifically minded spoilsports have been quick to point out that the Devilsbit is composed entirely of sandstone while the Rock of Cashel is a limestone outcrop. Nevertheless, the mountain offers a

Sunset at the Devilsbit Gap (Courtesy C. Needham)

charming walk with great views and many other evocative resonances for those who enjoy an easier outing with many historic echoes.

From your parking place, **S043 730**, walk for a leisurely 20 minutes or so, keeping to the left option where the track divides until an obvious T-junction is reached. Go right and follow around to the south side of the mountain and continue until you notice a prominent round tower on your right. This is not a round tower of monastic origin, as you might at first suspect, but an eighteenth-century folly built by the wealthy landowning Carden family of Templemore.

The folly was, however, used as the site for a monster meeting in 1832, when, according to local folklore, Ireland's Liberator, Daniel O'Connell, addressed an assembled multitude of 50,000. At the time he was campaigning against the compulsory payment of tithes to the established Church but, nevertheless, some modern-day historians doubt that he was personally present on the occasion.

If he did attend, however, he spoke in English. A fluent Irish speaker, he nevertheless tended to address meetings in English to ensure that the newspapers of the day would print his words. The downside was, of course, that in this way he unwittingly contributed further to the rapid decline of spoken Irish, which took place during the nineteenth century.

At this point, go left and follow the track steeply upwards. To your right you will pass an altar and shrine. On a late July Sunday each year – known locally as Rock Sunday – the shrine here is the scene for the celebration of Mass. This is just one example of the long-standing tradition of pattern-day pilgrimages, which take place annually on many other mountains across Ireland and are, for the most part, examples of the Christianisation of earlier pagan worship.

Continue upwards and you are soon within the actual gap that forms the Devilsbit proper. Disappointingly this turns out to be just a rather mundane col, but the sense of history is maintained by the fact that it was on a ledge in the nearby cliffs that the priceless Book of Dimma was reputedly discovered. This is a beautifully illuminated eighth-century gospel created at nearby St Cronan's Abbey, Roscrea, which now resides in the National Museum, Dublin.

Now square your shoulders and head left towards the summit of what is known locally as the Little Rock. A short, but steep, scramble past a statue of the Blessed Virgin is required to reach the actual top, which is crowned by a large cross that was built to celebrate the Marian Year of 1954 and is now spectacularly floodlit by night. Here you are rewarded with views to Lough Derg and the Slieve Bloom Mountains, while to the south you gaze across the fertile plains of Tipperary bounded in the far distance by the great upland ring consisting of the Galtee, Comeragh and Knockmealdown Mountains.

Descend from the mountaintop by an alternative track on the opposite side from which you approached the summit. This track first skirts a forest on the left and then swings round to enter a wood, before joining a wider track. Go left at this point and continue until you reach the three-way junction encountered earlier. Here a right turn brings you back to your car having enjoyed an exhilarating but not overly demanding outing.

Longer route

If you prefer a longer outing you can extend your walk by retracing your steps from the Marian Year Cross to the Devilsbit Gap and then following a track that ascends to a plateau known as the Long Rock, which in recent years has become an occasional playground for rock climbers. Continue through heathery terrain to the trig point that represents the summit of Devilsbit Mountain proper (480m) before descending steeply from the plateau. Next follow a rough track with forestry to your left until it joins a green road leading through a gate near a large communications mast. Swing left here and return along a forest roadway that leads you back to the original T–junction from where it is a 20-minute stroll to your start point. This will allow you the time to reflect, perhaps, that the Devilsbit is a classic example of an 'espresso mountain' – small in stature, but packing quite a punch.

WALK 23
PORTUMNA FOREST PARK

START:
The start point is from the car park of the Shannon Oaks Hotel & Country Club, which is situated just outside the village of Portumna, County Galway, close to the junction with the N65 Loughrea road.

Time:
3 hours.

Map:
OSi Sheet 53 (not necessary, as the circuit is clearly waymarked).

Suitability:
This is a low-level walk containing almost nothing in terms of hills and no special skills are required to complete it. Just follow the directions above from the Shannon Oaks Hotel to the trailhead. Then be led by the red arrows denoting the Bonaveen Loop.

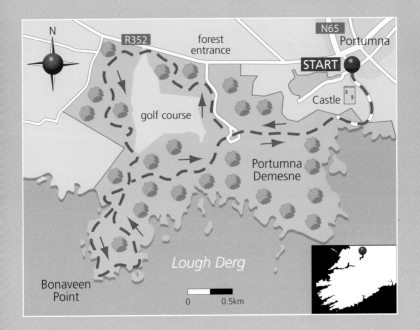

Portumna Forest Park

OK, OK! Before you dash off a letter of complaint to the publisher, my hands are up – Portumna is not in east Munster and for that matter it isn't exactly an upland area either. But then Galway isn't a Leinster hurling county, the 'Fields of Athenry' isn't a Munster song and Eamon de Valera wasn't even a native-born Irishman. Life is full of ambiguity and it seems churlish to exclude one of my favourite low-level circuits, suitable for all the family, just because it lies a couple of kilometres on the Connacht side of the Shannon.

So firm your resolve and head bravely into the West to enjoy a memorable outing starting from the Shannon Oaks Hotel at **N850 044**. First ramble the evocative Yew Walk where branches neatly intertwine overhead to reach the gates of tastefully restored Portumna Castle. This imposing fortified house built by Richard De Burgo, was the family seat of the Clanricarde Earls for two centuries and it is well worth taking a diversion here for a guided tour of the castle during its summertime opening period.

Follow the trail beside the exterior castle walls leading to a picturesque marina. Then continue along the trail past an area of cleared forest, which is being carefully restored to oak, ash and hazel woodland as part of an admirable native trees preservation scheme. Soon afterwards, a right fork in the path leads to the main trailhead for the forest park walks where there are map boards, toilets, car parking and picnic tables. At weekends this is usually a busy place with an assorted collection of walkers, bikers, buggy strollers, joggers and amblers – all enjoying a welcome opportunity for a down-time reconciliation with nature.

The River Shannon in evening twilight

Opt here for the Bonaveen Trail, which is billed the longest and most picturesque loop walk and is denoted with red arrows. This kicks off along narrow woodland paths that are excellently maintained by Coillte with an absence of those vertigo-inducing tubular metal stiles, which are now common on many Irish walkways. Instead there are wooden swinging gates along with boardwalks and tiny well-constructed bridges that fit neatly into the landscape.

The trail now passes Portumna Golf Club – where it is possible to pop in for a coffee and a snack if the mood takes you. Next continue through pleasant mixed woodlands before passing a forest-enclosed turlough. This is a lake that disappears when the water table falls in summer only to reappear in winter, with this particular one then providing a welcome sanctuary for an abundance of waterfowl. Turloughs are a feature typical of low-lying limestone areas and most turloughs in Ireland are found west of the River Shannon.

Eventually you return briefly to a forestry road before heading off again on a series of narrow trails leading to Bonaveen Point. This is, at once, the high point and the lowest point of the walk with the quicksilver waters of the Shannon sparkling vividly through the trees creating an evocative landscape. This low-lying area exudes with stay-a-while charm and makes an ideal place for a food break.

Soon after, you come to a clearing where it is common to see fallow deer grazing nonchalantly while above noisy squirrels inhabit the tree-lined canopy. In such circumstances time passes by on slow-motion wings and so, in what seems no length of time, you will suddenly re-emerge at the trailhead. From here simply retrace your steps past the marina and castle back to the car park of the Shannon Oaks Hotel.